CLASSIC TRAINS

CLASSIC TRAINS

NICHOLAS FAITH

BOXTREE

In Association with Channel Four Television Corporation

This paperback edition published in Great Britain in 1998 by Boxtree

First published in Great Britain in 1997 by Boxtree
an imprint of Macmillan Publishers Ltd
25 Eccleston Place, London, SW1W 9NF

Associated companies throughout the world

ISBN 0 7522 1160 9

1 3 5 7 9 10 8 6 4 2

A CIP catalogue entry for this book is available from the British Library.

Designed by Robert Updegraff
Printed and bound in Italy

Half title page: *A steam tram of the North London Tramways in the 1880s.*
Title page: *One of the famous series of Pacific locomotives. This one, number 4468, was named after its designer, Sir Nigel Gresley.*

Classic Trains accompanies the Channel 4 series 'Classic Trains' produced by Uden Associates.

CONTENTS

Acknowledgements

Like its predecessors, *Classic Trucks* and *Classic Ships*, this book was made possible by Peter Grimsdale and Susanna Yager at Channel 4 and by their confidence that I could write it in the short time available. As with previous books, the team responsible for the television series of the same name at Patrick Uden Associates – Michael Proudfoot, Stewart Sugg, Chris Durlacher, James Castle, Alison Dillon, Natasha Bondy, Gaby Franklin and Gemma Chapman – somehow found time to be more helpful than I had any right to expect. At Boxtree, Susanna Wadeson, the solicitous Katy Carrington and that *non pareil* of copy editors, Caroline North, did wonders – their efforts were almost transcended by the speed with which Robert Updegraff produced an elegant design. Thank you all.

Following spread: **The Welshpool and Llanfair Railway (2'6" gauge) special train run for members of the Locomotive Club of Great Britain.**

Classic Trains

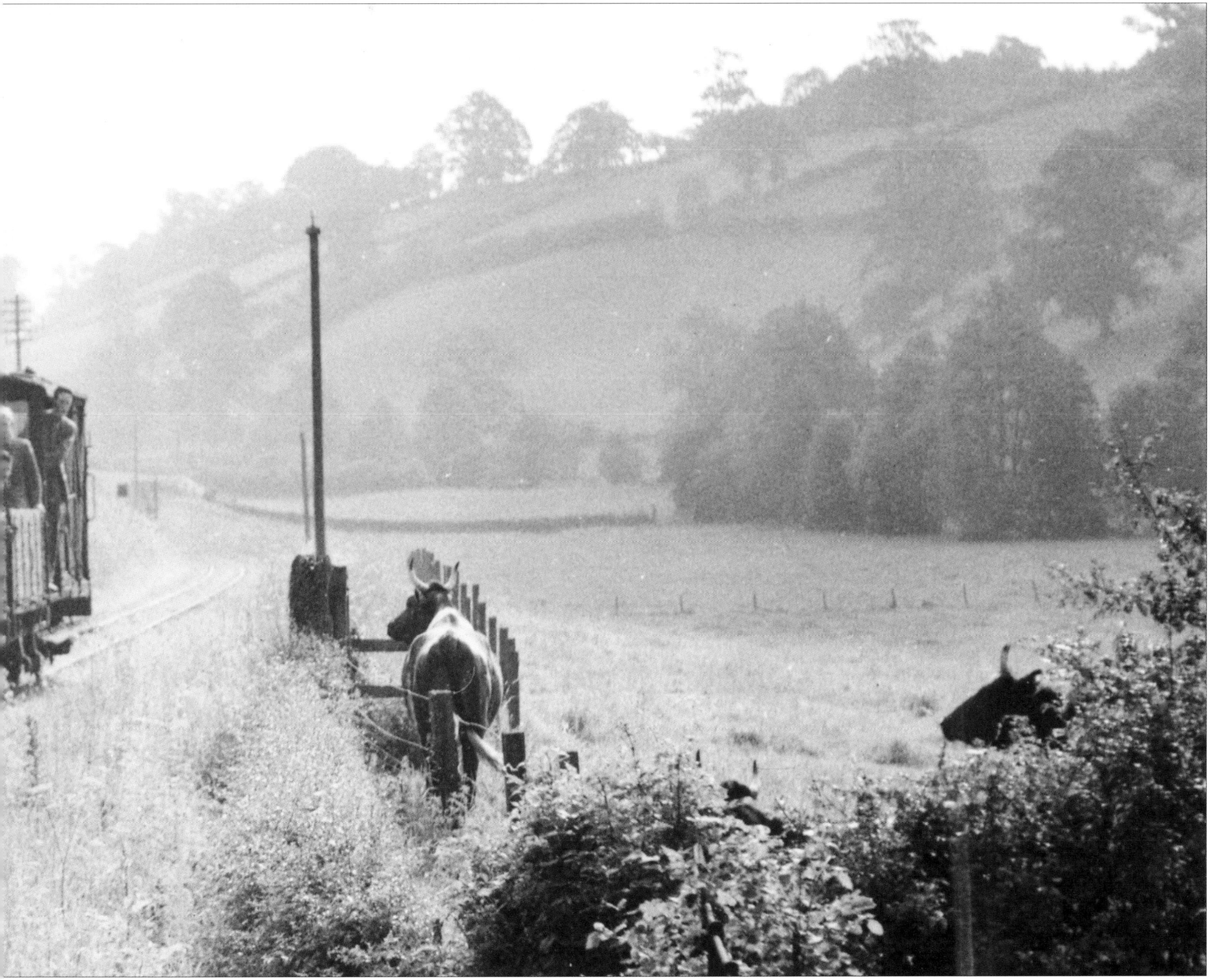

CHAPTER ONE

RETURN TRAIN

RAILWAYS ARE BACK. In the past few years people – and governments – the world over have begun to realize that they are the only environmentally friendly means of mass transport for passengers and freight. The social and environmental cost of the unrestricted use of motor vehicles, and the sheer congestion it causes, have led to a swing back to what was decried in the postwar decades as an outmoded system, doomed to be superseded by the all-conquering motor.

The re-emergence of railways echoes the way in which they created the modern world in the nineteenth century. Nations such as Belgium, Italy and Canada could not have existed without them; empires steamed along the lines built by the conquerors. They defied distance, they liberated man's imagination. The industrial revolution depended on them: trains were the only method of transporting the vast quantities of food required to feed the world's growing cities. They made possible the mass movement of people, first emigrants and later tourists. Railway stations were aptly known as 'temples of steam', and many remain among the finest monuments to the Victorian age.

Then and now, railway systems are an indication of a country's capacity to organize its transport systems, and thus, by implication, other less visible infrastructures, in a sane, economic and socially responsible manner. It has often been said that newspapers represent a nation talking to itself. Similarly, railways are a manifestation of a society, a community, in motion. As Paul Theroux puts it in *The Old Patagonian Express*, railways continue to provide an accurate reflection of the moral, cultural, social and economic state of a country. 'The seedy, distressed country has seedy, distressed trains; the proud, efficient nation is similarly reflected in its rolling stock, as Japan is. There is hope in India because the trains are considered vastly more important than the monkey wagons some Indians drive.'

Today most countries in the developed world are striving towards the better society represented by a superior railway system and are prepared to pay for the benefits. Every European government, with the sole exception of Britain, is investing heavily in existing rail systems, some neglected for a generation, most hitherto strangled in a web of bureaucracy. Yet after the Second World War railways seemed doomed to play an ever-decreasing role in people's lives. Throughout the world, institutional rigidities prevented them from adapting to challenge the increasing domination of the car, the lorry and the bus.

Thirty years ago the late Louis Armand, the chairman of the French network SNCF and the greatest of postwar railwaymen, prophesied that the railway would become the prime transport medium of the twenty-first century, as it had been in the nineteenth. At the time he was thought wrong, if not slightly unhinged, for the triumph of the internal combustion engine – of the car, the coach and the truck – seemed permanent. For over fifty years – between the end of

God bless you Ma'am. Queen Victoria, a firm fan of railways, at Gosport near Portsmouth, greeting King Louis Philippe of France in 1844, four years before he was dethroned by his ungrateful subjects.

the First World War and the oil crisis of 1973 which first jolted the complacency of the motor-mad – its advance had appeared irresistible: the motor car spelled individual freedom and the lorry provided the same flexibility for businesses, enabling them to provide services and deliver goods without having to depend on the usually unreliable rail services. In the event Armand has been proved right. We have long since passed the point when motor vehicles were deemed automatically desirable as the environment, and social factors of all kinds, compound the growing disenchantment with the privately owned motor vehicle.

Yet miraculously, trains are recognizably the same means of transport as those first developed to carry coal between mines, rivers and the sea in north-east England in the 1820s. The TGVs (an abbreviation of *trains à grande vitesse*, or high-speed trains) hurtling throughout France at 200mph (322kph) still depend on steel wheels running on steel rails set, as in George Stephenson's day, 4ft 8½ins (1,435mm) apart and using the electric motors first developed by Dr Siemens over a century ago.

The most visible sign of the railways' comeback is the ever-increasing railway-connected building throughout the world, and some of the most exciting developments are happening beyond the gaze of Eurocentrics. With extraordinary, almost imperial boldness, the Iranians have just opened a new link enabling Muslim central Asia to transport goods and passengers not northwards towards their former masters in Moscow, but south to the Persian Gulf. In the longer run they are hoping to recreate, in the form of a continuous railway link, the Great Silk Road between Europe and China, the fabled route of the Middle Ages which brought all the wonders of the East westward to barbaric Europe. It is quite possible that within a decade there will be two separate land bridges between Europe and China, one using the Trans-Siberian railway, and the other linking Turkey, Iran and Kasakhstan to western China. Already adventurous tour companies are running trains from Paris to southern China, Hong Kong and even Saigon.

Crossing the estuary at Barmouth on a romantic line along the Welsh coast which has always been unprofitable, yet survives because of its beauty and the strength of local feeling.

The most well publicized and technologically advanced schemes have naturally seen the light of day in more industrially developed countries. The pattern was set as far back as 1964, when the Japanese struck the first blow with the construction of the first Shinkansen, or 'bullet train'. Their example has been followed throughout the region: Asian 'tigers' like Taiwan and South Korea are building their own high-speed lines, while the Chinese are planning one between Shanghai and Beijing. China is also continuing with a building programme of more new standard lines of breathtaking scope and boldness. Europe now has the Channel Tunnel, and others are being built between Denmark and Sweden. There are high-speed lines in France, Germany, Italy and Spain, while more are being constructed throughout western Europe as far east as Russia, where plans for a new high-speed link between Moscow and St Petersburg are well advanced.

Yet because of the power of the road lobby – not to mention petty nationalistic jealousies – western Europe's railways are not carrying nearly as much freight as they could. Here the pace is being set in the United States, a country where, until 1979, trains averaged a mere 11mph (17.7kph) – a result of the regulatory strait jacket imposed nearly 100 years earlier, before the advent of the internal combustion engine, when the railways held, and exploited, a virtual monopoly of land travel. In the past decade and a half they have fought back, recapturing much of the long-haul business for carrying freight over 500 miles (805km) – an example which could be copied in Europe were individual railway organizations prepared to co-operate.

So how does Britain fare in the international league table? To put it bluntly, as a country which is slipping towards the Third World or, perhaps more accurately, a country which has for a long time lacked vision and resigned itself to mediocrity, to a 'making do' and 'muddling through' approach, for its attitude to the management of its railway system is characteristic of so many other aspects of its national life. With a handful of exceptions – notably the London Underground in the 1930s and the electrification of the West Coast Main Line between London and Scotland in the late 1950s and early 1960s – Britain seems to have lacked the capacity to envisage, plan and execute any bold new initiatives; to have been unwilling to set the pace.

The West Coast Main Line between London, Birmingham, Manchester and Liverpool – built in the 1830s within a decade of the opening of the Liverpool to Manchester railway – was the first rail system in the world to link major cities more than a few miles apart. It is going to take far longer to rejuvenate the line than it took to build it – and it is all too likely that the British will end up accepting a botch-up, a railway operating less effectively and at lower speeds than the main arteries in any other industrially developed country. Inevitably, perhaps, the biggest contribution of British railways since the war has been an intellectual one: the concept of InterCity, that the fastest trains should not be 'specials' confined to passengers prepared to pay a premium, but should be regular services available at the same price as the lower-grade ones.

In spite of its lack of progress, British Rail had been universally admired by railwaymen outside Britain for managing to provide services varying between the reasonable and the excellent under an appalling financial regime which combined minimal government support and a total inability to take a long-term view. This latter point is essential, since Britain still relies on a mainline network which, as we shall see in Chapters 3 and 4, was largely completed by 1852.

The British approach is in marked contrast to that of the French. They now have a major network of TGVs, new lines on which trains travel regularly, without any fuss, at between 150mph and 200mph (241–322kph) day in, day out, using technical equipment, which, apart from a signalling system controlled from the driver's cab, would be recognizable to previous generations of railwaymen. However, the project has been achieved at a cost – and not only in the enormous burden of debt accumulated by the SNCF. The focus on the TGV system has led to a large-scale neglect of the rest of the rail system and an inability to provide a regular service on more ordinary lines, or to exploit the minor rural branches

A dream come true. A Eurostar train about to set off for Paris, pictured in the dappled sunlight at the magnificent new Waterloo International Station.

which extend from the many stations lucky enough to be served by TGVs. By contrast, before it was broken up by the ideological fanatics of John Major's government, BR had demonstrated how electrically or diesel-powered 'rail buses' (in railway jargon, DMUs or EMUs – diesel or electrical multiple units) could provide regular services at reasonable, if not exciting, speeds between innumerable towns and cities, sometimes on routes that would appear unprofitable to the outsider, like that between Norwich and Liverpool. The idea is sensible, forward-looking and intellectually imaginative, producing services of considerable value to the communities served, and taking advantage of a major technical

The – it must be admitted rather unromantic – view from the observation car at the rear of the LNER's 1937 _Coronation Train_.

advance: new diesels which are both powerful and relatively quiet. In one important sense, DMUs and EMUs represent the future for railways: a new-found flexibility. They are a typically British triumph: a second-best notion, using existing lines to their fullest extent, without incurring any great expenditure (although more will be needed on the track and signalling if the trains are to be able to run at their design speed, which is often 90mph [145kph]). Yet the British do not make a fuss about rail buses.

This is symptomatic of an overall incapacity to rejoice in our genuine achievements or to contemplate any concerted effort to exploit railways more systematically. Britain, a crowded island eminently suited to rail travel, is the only country outside the United States which remains unable to contemplate abolishing the subsidies given to road transport in the form of company-car allowances, ludicrously low taxation of heavy lorries and relatively cheap petrol. Privatization, the Conservative government's magic cure-all, is simply a pathetic attempt to evade society's responsibilities towards its transport systems; indeed, it is a denial of the idea of society, of the community on the move.

Because of this lack of what ex-President Bush famously called 'the vision thing', the British national tendency, in railway matters as in so many other respects, is to hark back rather than to look forward. It is crucially important, then, for the author of a book accompanying a television series called 'Classic Trains' not to wallow in the past, for there have already been too many books and television programmes inviting nostalgic Brits to wallow in the contemplation of the generally slow, dirty and unreliable steam engines. Instead I have taken each of the themes the programmes focus on and have tried to encourage British rail-lovers, who tend to be happiest when they are at their most nostalgic, to look forward; to acknowledge that there are such things as modern classics – developments which echo the triumphs of the past but at the same time point ahead. Doubters need only turn to Chapter 8 to see how the beloved old tram has been successfully resurrected under the trendier nomenclature of 'light railway'. Or perhaps they should pay a visit to Nicholas Grimshaw's Waterloo International Station, a modern masterpiece fit to stand with those built in London 100 years earlier.

CHAPTER TWO

WHY RAILWAYS?

WHY EXACTLY DO WE need railways today? It's one of those seemingly childish questions which should nag at everyone who cares about them. The answer, briefly, is that in the modern world, assuming that we are talking about a country which has properly developed systems of motorways and domestic air transport, railways remain totally indispensable in cities, towns and conurbations. Moreover, they are competitive in two other situations: with air travel in transporting passengers on journeys of up to three hours (four if the passengers are not interested merely in speed but in comfort and convenience as well), and with road transport in carrying freight over a certain distance (which can range from 500 miles [305km] for general freight to less than 200 [322km] when it comes to bulk loads like coal and building materials). It is surely the task of governments to establish that most elusive of settings, the 'level playing field' in which railways can make their biggest possible contribution, by providing them with the requisite finance – including long-term capital.

It is manifestly absurd to expect the railway infrastructure to make a profit if it is to compete effectively with an untaxed road system. Yet in Britain, Railtrack, as a privatized industry, is required to do precisely that. The only argument, though it is a strong one, in favour of privatization in this case was that it was the only way to release the track and stations from the grip of the Treasury, whose obsession with short-term financial considerations was so entrenched that any form of long-term investment was almost impossible.

Yet because the railways have been an apparently immutable part of our lives, our landscapes, for so long, we seem to have neglected to question how they should be developed. For too many years they have been left by the governments in many countries – and not only in Europe – in the hands of those who run them, and these managers have naturally evolved either into bureaucrats concerned with their own status and comfort rather than the welfare of the system for which they are responsible, or, more often, into train operators, men (virtually no women have ever been involved) playing at trains without paying too much attention to the finances or the interests of the passengers. Yet for every puffed-up paper-pusher or small boy playing with his train set there were 100 dedicated railwaymen keeping their system going in the face of government meanness and shortsightedness.

One man, almost inevitably an outsider, who did try to plan for the future, at least as far as Britain was concerned, was the late and unjustly reviled Dr Richard, later Lord, Beeching, the chairman of British Rail in the early 1960s. Over a quarter of a century after he left BR, his name is still attached by self-proclaimed rail-lovers to the policy of wholesale slaughter of railway services. In reality, Beeching was the only man since the war with the vision and the managerial and intellectual equipment to provide Britain with an efficient system attuned to the country's social and economic needs. Indeed, he was the very model of the sort of public-sector manager so common in France and so rare on the other side of the Channel.

Pamela Cornell's romantic view of an express train complete with advertising posters for chocolate and, at the left, a railway official who looks like something out of the adventures of Babar the Elephant.

Beeching's philosophy was simplicity itself. As he once told a group of railwaymen:

> I see the railways as a national asset, owned by the nation and therefore to be used in the best interest of the nation as a whole . . . My job and that of the British Railways Board is to run the railways in the best interests of the whole community. To do this we have to strive for conditions of service and pay which satisfy our staff; we have to provide a quality and cost of service which satisfies our customers and we have to do this without imposing an intolerable cost burden on the country as a whole.

A forgotten pioneer, the little line from Canterbury to Whitstable on the Kent coast, was opened as early as 1830.

Beeching was a brilliant physicist who became deputy chief engineer of armament design at the War Office in his early thirties and technical director of ICI at the age of forty. His appointment to the chairmanship of British Rail was controversial because he insisted on being paid the same salary he had enjoyed at ICI (a then-colossal £24,000 [$36,000]). The ensuing row concealed unease within the establishment at the very idea of managerial competence being deployed to solve a public-sector problem, a solution so alien to the historic British love of muddle.

Beeching brought considerable personal qualities to his task. Firm, determined and courteous, he was also wily. If you have a sticky problem, he once told a colleague, 'work

This delightful painting by the unjustly neglected artist Eric Ravilious enshrines the essentially English notion of even *real* trains as picturesque toys.

out an answer, create chaos and then offer up the solution'. Unlike many meritocrats he also had a sense of humour (he once annotated some graffiti in a station lavatory which stated 'Beeching is a prat' by adding a firm, 'No, I'm not'). He was a true intellectual always prepared to argue his case, which was simplicity itself. When he arrived at BR he was staggered by the complete absence of statistical analysis and financial awareness. The most straightforward figures showed that half of BR's 7,000 stations processed a mere 2 per cent of its total traffic. At a time when car ownership was rapidly increasing, it was ridiculous to suppose that all 3,500 of these could be worth preserving. But inevitably, his restructuring plans – designed not as a firm blueprint but as a basis for the public interest to be measured in financial terms (then in itself a revolutionary concept) – were greeted with hysterical opposition.

Beeching's detractors refused to accept his concept of dividing the railways into the economic commercial sector,

Opposite: **The *West Highlander* express steaming across the Glenfinnan viaduct on the far reaches of the romantic line between Fort William and Mallaig.**

Right: **One of the most striking (and valuable) of the railway posters commissioned by major railway companies between the wars. This image of the *Flying Scotsman* by the famous Russian-born artist Alexandre Alexeieff is now worth over £10,000.**

THE NIGHT SCOTSMAN
Leaves King's Cross nightly at 10.25.

which he was prepared to run without subsidy, and the more numerous remaining services, which required government support. This demanded a series of decisions from government on the social and practical necessity for specific services – the sort of choices governments hate to make. It also required the development and implementation of a proper cost-benefit analysis comparing road with rail transport, taking into account all the evils, direct and indirect, created by road traffic, and the degree to which road transport, of both freight and passengers, was subsidized.

Beeching accepted the point that, in western Europe at least, the majority of railway services would never be able to make enough profit to satisfy normal investment criteria, and that the rationale for their existence must always include a strong element of public good. In somewhere like the United States services make money because they are almost exclusively devoted to carrying freight over long distances, generally measured in thousands rather than hundreds of miles. By contrast, apart from metro services in and around major cities and a single line between New York and Washington, there is effectively no such thing as a regular passenger train service in that whole vast country.

It requires breadth of imagination to envisage a long-term balance sheet for a railway system. Lester Thurow, a well-known economist at the Massachusetts Institute of Technology (MIT), once likened transportation to education:

> Suppose I was a hard-nosed capitalist mother and father thinking about sending my children for sixteen years' worth of education. That is a lousy investment that no capitalist would ever make. What, sixteen years with no returns? There isn't any way it could pay off. On the other hand, having an educated population does pay off for every society. And the same thing is true for a good transportation system. If you look at it in any moment in time, and judge it in very narrow criteria, it probably doesn't make sense . . . On the other hand, in the long run it does. It's the thing that holds us together, the transportation system.

In Britain, as in many other countries, the decline in the commercial viability of the railway system predated the arrival of the internal combustion engine. As we shall see in Chapters 3 and 4, during the nineteenth century railways made numerous fortunes for a variety of people, by no means all of them criminal, and even showed some profit for some canny investors. But by 1900 they were losing their attractiveness as financial investments. In *Howards End*, one of E. M. Forster's characters shows her independence of spirit by investing in 'foreign things which always smash', rather than in the fictional Nottingham & Derby, a supposedly safer domestic rail company. Irritatingly, however, the 'foreign things' did admirably, while the Nottingham and Derby 'declined with the steady dignity of which only home rails are

capable'. The historian T. R. Gourvish, confirms the novelist's insight here, attributing the deterioration partly to the continuing obsession of successive governments with curbing the power and profits of the railway companies. As early as 1900, he wrote, 'It was clear that the railway companies' freedom to choose and charge the traffic they carried had been severely restricted by legislation designed to encourage a "public service" obligation in management.'[1] In the absence of any real competition, the railways could just about survive, although their shareholders were rewarded only with steadily decreasing profits.

But the railways emerged from the First World War so weakened that in 1923 the government forced them to amalgamate into four groups, each with their regional monopolies: the Great Western, the Southern, the London Midland and Scottish, and the London and North-Eastern. This decision signalled the abandonment of any serious attempt to encourage competition, a lesson John Major's government ignored when it reprivatized the industry and tried, unsuccessfully, to reintroduce a competitive element into the system. But even this monopoly did not prevent the erosion of profit margins to minimal or non-existent levels. Two forces were at work on freight traffic, generally reckoned to be the most profitable element of the business: ever-increasing competition from the flexible motor lorry was the most obvious, but in addition the decline of Britain's heavy industries was reducing the base

This rather surreal image was captured when the first trains on the Victoria Line were opened for inspection by the press in February 1968.

loads – coal, minerals, iron and steel – which had proved such reliable staples in the past. Even in the recovery years of the late 1930s, production of coal, for instance, was 16 per cent below that of 1913.

Yet the government persisted in treating the railways as though they still retained their former monopoly of inland transport. In spite of the justified protests of the railway companies their rates were still regulated. Any attempt to avoid the regulations was stamped on, although the railways' attempt to get a 'square deal' might have been successful had another war not broken out in September 1939. The steadily worsening financial situation was reflected in the dividends. In the 1930s the GWR had to pay theirs partly out of reserves, the LMS reduced its dividend, while the LNER paid nothing on its 5 per cent preferred ordinary shares in the four years before the war. Only the Southern increased its dividend, thanks to the electrification programme described in Chapter 7 and to its other interests (its ports, especially Dover and Southampton, and its fleet of ships were so profitable that the Southern was once described as a docks and shipping business that also ran a railway). In addition, the Southern was the only group to respond to its financial difficulties by trying to increase services, running its rolling stock flat out from 5am to well past midnight.

The four groups were partly responsible for their own problems. Their management was complacent; in-grown, with few if any breaths of fresh air (one of the few was Lord Stamp, the statistician who forced the LMS to build more powerful locomotives because they were more economical). They also retained until well after nationalization the almost tribal loyalties towards their railway displayed by employees of the component companies.

In almost fifty years of public ownership after the railways were nationalized in 1948, not a single government proved capable of establishing a proper balance between long-term investment, financial control and wider transport considerations. The two major investment programmes – the modernization plan of the late 1950s and early 1960s and a burst in the mid-1980s – were the result of one-off bargains between the governments of the day and BR chairmen. In the first instance Sir Brian Robertson simply said that if you wanted to modernize you had to provide the finance, while in 1980 Sir Robert Reid (the first of two successive chairmen of the same name) did a deal with the secretary of transport, the late Nicholas Ridley, which allowed him to invest in the system the proceeds from the development of BR's extensive property portfolio.

In the short term the privatization programme of the Major government was a doomed attempt to introduce some element of competition and to force everyone to compete for resources in the maze of the 130 companies into which British Rail was broken up. The cost was enormous – around £1 billion ($1.5 billion) in fees, and up to ten times that amount in assets sold at below their true value to the private sector. Inevitably, as happened with other utilities, no sooner had parts of the system been privatized than they started to come together again in the form of bids for one type of company for another, most obviously the bid for the Porterbrook rolling stock leasing company by the bus giant Stagecoach.

Nevertheless, although it is too soon yet to tell, in the longer run the whole, apparently wasteful and pointless exercise could do some good. It could establish the limits to which even (some would say especially) privately run railways can do without public subsidy. It could provide a boost to Britain's rail-freight traffic, albeit only because, in defiance of the government's declared policy, a single company, the American Wisconsin Central, run by a forward-looking entrepreneur, Ed Burckhardt, was allowed to take over all three of BR's freight companies. And, most importantly, it removes control of the whole rail system from the dead hand of the Treasury. There could be worse fates for a much-abused rail system than a series of monopoly services, provided that they are forced to carry out the conditions laid out in their franchising agreements, and to stretch further the still underexploited possibilities of rail travel in Britain – and provided, too, that the bodies that regulate them use their powers for the public good and not, as has happened with many other privatized utilities, for the good of fat-cat directors. A slim hope, perhaps.

Old Locomotive Engine
Wylam Coll.

Thos. H. Hair.

CHAPTER THREE

THE PIONEERS

T HE IDEA OF A RAILWAY was nothing new. For hundreds of years horse-drawn carts had used tracked routes to carry coal in mines or from them to the nearest navigable waters. But it was not until the first couple of decades of the nineteenth century that British engineers triumphantly demonstrated that steam locomotives could provide adequate power to propel economic loads of passengers or freight along a rail.

The road which led to the opening of the Liverpool to Manchester Railway in 1830, the convincing proof of the success of their efforts, was a long one, and the final achievement of a steam-powered locomotive running on iron rails was by no means a foregone conclusion. The railway needed a whole host of technical developments – the rails had to be strong enough to support a steam engine, and the engine in turn had to be compact enough to be mobile and able to deliver reliable power. Finally, and crucially, the railway had to be economic. It required a base load on which it could rely to service the unprecedented amount of capital it took to build (and remember that there could be no income at all until the whole system was in place).

It was no coincidence that the modern railway was born in the north-east of England, which can be compared with the other regions – notably and most recently Silicon Valley in California – which bring together the resources required to spearhead the development of the major new technology of the day. In the first decades of the nineteenth century the

area that is now Tyne and Wear contained a concentration of mines, of railways – and thus of capital – unique in Britain and therefore in the world, for Britain was, and was to remain for several more decades, virtually the only country which was industrializing itself.

While Silicon Valley, as its name declares, is based on the computer chip, the north-east of England was founded on a more natural asset: coal. As a government official, Captain J. M. Laws, said in 1845: 'We owe all our railways to the collieries of the north; and the difficulties which their industry overcame taught us to make railways and to make locomotives to run on them.' [1] The combination of rapidly disappearing forests and the growing requirements of industry, and of the fireplaces of a burgeoning capital, led to an ever-increasing demand for coal, which was principally supplied by the north-east, from where it could easily be carried by sea from the Tyne to London. Getting it from the mine to the quay was another matter: the country was simply too rugged for the construction of the canals in use elsewhere in England. The answer was 'wagon ways', parallel sets of rails made initially of wood, later of iron, leading from the pit down to navigable water. These provided the horses with a smoother road on which they could haul larger loads uphill, the journey downwards generally relying on gravity.

The development of a steam engine which could be mounted on a locomotive took over a century. The first steam engines, used to pump water out of mines, were developed in

An evocative, almost Impressionistic, image from the pre-history of steam locomotion: an old engine at Wylam Colliery painted by Thomas Hair in the 1840s.

A prototype of the 'rail-way', a Newcastle 'Chaldron' or coal wagon running along an iron-way as early as 1746.

Opposite: **London's first railway, the demonstration track rigged up by the Cornish engineer Richard Trevithick in 1809 in Eaton Square, heart of now ultra-fashionable Belgravia.**

the early years of the eighteenth century. Sixty years later, James Watt produced an engine which could turn wheels and mobile steam power became a technical possibility. But Watt was not interested in mobile engines, and the further development of steam engines had to wait for the expiry of his patents in 1800.

But one man had not waited. By 1797, Richard Trevithick, son of the manager of a tin mine in Cornwall, had developed a 'strong steam' engine, that is, one with relatively high pressure which let the steam out directly into the atmosphere, thus eliminating the need for a condenser, avoiding Watt's patents and creating the puffing noise characteristic of steam engines from that day on. As John Ransom points out, in building his first non-condensing engine Trevithick 'had grasped another vital point: that a steam engine using strong steam could, with a boiler, be made far more compact than existing beam engines. It could be compact enough to power a carriage.'[2]

Trevithick was not the only, or even the first inventor to have discovered this. Two Frenchmen, N. J. Cugnot and the Marquis Jourfrroy d'Abbans, had already built mobile steam engines, and in the first decade of the nineteenth century the steam-powered boat was being developed in the United States. In the 1780s William Murdock, Watt's leading engineer, had produced a steam-driven vehicle but had been persuaded by his employer to abandon the project.

In the face of fierce hostility from the manufacturers of low-pressure steam engines, Trevithick went on to introduce the horizontal boiler, which could be stronger and thus produce steam at a higher pressure than its vertical equivalent, and by 1803 he had built a steam carriage which transported 10 tons of iron on a wagon way in South Wales. Unfortunately, Trevithick was relying on rails too brittle for the weight of his carriage, and he also lacked the technical and financial backing available in the north-east, where a

J Rowlandson

number of engineers were already at work along the same lines, as it were. By 1813 William Hedley had built *Puffing Billy* (and *Wylam Dilly*, named after his colliery) and proved that it was more efficient for an engine to run on smooth rails rather than, as was supposed at the time, on a rack rail.

During the thirty years which culminated in the opening of the Stockton and Darlington Railway in 1824, all the strands were coming into place. In 1795 the long brake was invented, allowing sets of wagons to descend steep gradients relatively safely. The narrow-gauge rail was introduced by William Jessop in 1789, this time in far-off Leicestershire. Over the years wrought iron became less brittle and there was a steady stream of improvements in the design of the rails, the chairs and the sleepers into which the chairs and the rails were set.

But to make a success of their enterprise the developers needed a favourable economic and political environment. Fortunately for them, the years after the end of the Napoleonic Wars in 1815 saw a rapid rise in the price of fodder, and thus of horsepower. As a result the replacement of animal by steam power seemed as much an economic as a technological triumph. Moreover, the resulting replacement of fodder with coal was a major step in freeing mankind from his dependence on the vagaries of nature.

In 1818 the great engineer Thomas Telford pronounced himself in favour of an iron way rather than a canal for the route which was later to become the Stockton and Darlington Railway, though his acceptance was qualified and carefully hedged. The country had to be rugged; the water necessary for locks lacking; the freight relatively heavy. All the same, Telford was thus acknowledging defeat. The railway-builders still depended on the techniques practised and experience gained from the large-scale construction work of the canal-builders. That same year George Overton, the builder of the tramways used by Trevithick, wrote: 'Railways are now generally adopted and the cutting of canals nearly discontinued.'

So by the early 1820s, steam power was clearly in the ascendant. The first application of power was through stationary engines at the top of an incline to which the wagons were hitched and it was not clear for another decade whether the engines would be mobile or stationary, hauling cable cars full of coal and passengers, for even George Stephenson was not yet totally committed to mobile-engine power.

There was even a visionary who projected the idea of a network of railways to replace the canals. He was William James, a man well placed to realize his ideas; indeed it was only a ruinous financial crisis in the early 1820s that prevented him from reaping the reward of his efforts. James was a distinguished land agent, and a multimillionaire in today's terms, by the middle of the second decade of the century. After failing to launch new canals or turnpike roads to transport the coal produced underneath his masters' lands, he came up with the idea of a railway system, centred on Birmingham, running from Liverpool and Wolverhampton to London. He also sketched a dozen other lines, notably from London to Brighton and Portsmouth and Chatham, which were all realized in the 1830s and 1840s.

More immediately he grasped the need for a railway connecting Liverpool with Manchester and other cotton towns to compete with the inordinately expensive Bridgewater Canal. In 1821 he formed a company to build the line, intended from the start to be powered by steam locomotives. At the time it was James, rather than the promoters of the Stockton and Darlington, who appeared best placed to exploit the locomotives Stephenson was producing.

He carried out a thorough survey of the line but when his company crashed the disaster took twenty years to sort out. James was pushed aside by Joseph Saunders, a local man to whom he had brought his ideas for the Liverpool–Manchester line. James died, a broken man, in 1837, but he was not forgotten. Nine years after his death, all the country's leading engineers (with the single exception of George Stephenson) formed a committee to compensate James's children for the fact that their father's 'successful exertions and great pecuniary sacrifices' had deprived his family of all patrimony. A letter spelled out the 'acknowledged fact that, to their father's labours, the public are indebted for the establishment of the present railroad system'.

This image of the opening of the Stockton to Darlington Railway in 1825 may look rather glamorised but does convey the feeling of how the train was an alien element in an otherwise unspoiled rural landscape.

As for George Stephenson, he could not bear the implication that he was not the sole creator of the railway. He was furious, and forced his son to withdraw his name from the letter. It complicated matters that James had been almost a second father to the young Robert Stephenson, who clearly found his real father an insupportable autocrat – he escaped to Latin America, where he spent some years seeking his fortune in the mines.

This shameful act was typical of the dark, arrogant side of George Stephenson, the man indissolubly, and rightly, associated with the achievements of the steam engine. To triumph against the doubters, the great majority of whom simply could not conceive of a means of transport not dependent on the power of man, horse or ox, took tremendous vision. Come the time, cometh the man. And the steam-powered railway duly produced its saviour.

Stephenson's success, like that of Winston Churchill more than a century later, was based on his character – on an obstinate determination, a steadfastness of purpose – as well as an element of being the right man in the right place at the right time. Like Churchill, Stephenson is honoured more in retrospect than he was during a long career largely spent battling the established order. 'Almost to a man,' wrote L. T. C. Rolt, 'his fellow engineers dismissed him as an

George Stephenson, rightly remembered as the Father of the World's Railways. But these careworn features covered a ruthless disposition.

unprincipled and incompetent schemer, but all their shafts broke against the armour of that stubborn determination to succeed which was to triumph over every obstacle, including his own weaknesses.'[3] As well as the arrogance displayed in Stephenson's attitude towards William James, these weaknesses included an almost pathological jealousy of other engineers, a completely autocratic nature and a profound managerial incompetence.

Yet the applause is not undeserved. In John Rowland's words, Stephenson 'did not originate the steam locomotive, he did not invent a new type of machine; but he used other people's inventions and improved them so completely as to make them peculiarly his own.'[4]

According to John Ransom, 'Among his improvements were direct drive from piston to wheel, coupling of wheels, slide valves worked by slip eccentrics and steam springs to support the weight of the boiler . . . he was the first to build a locomotive driven by adhesion, and carried on flange wheels which ran on edge rails.'[5] This arrangement became the conventional one, remains so to this day and indeed will do for the foreseeable future.

In some ways Stephenson was relatively conservative, notably and influentially in following historic precedent with the gauge of the railways he built. For centuries, some say since Roman times, mining engineers had been accustomed to railways laid to a gauge of about 4ft 8½ins (1,435mm). The reasons behind this specification remain obscure, but my guess would be that it was the narrowest that allowed horses to fit between the shafts of a cart or carriage. George Stephenson followed the tradition, using this gauge for the Stockton and Darlington and, for some unknown reason, adding an extra half-inch when he came to construct the Liverpool–Manchester line. The Stephensons effectively institutionalized the gauge, since their Newcastle factory dominated locomotive-building in Britain and manufactured the first engines to be seen in a dozen countries. Stephenson later claimed that he had originally preferred a 5ft 2ins (1,575mm) gauge but had reverted to the customary measure after discussing the matter with his son. Indeed, most of the

other major engineers at the time favoured a slightly broader gauge of between 5ft (1,524mm) and 5ft 6ins (1,676mm). They needed room for the biggest possible boilers and were looking for the lowest possible centre of gravity, both of which were facilitated by a broader gauge.

Stephenson enjoyed advantages unavailable to Trevithick who, in distant Cornwall, lacked the critical technical, financial and commercial resources to be found in the north-east. Stephenson had lived almost all his life on a tramway line, and he was able to draw on the experience of dozens of colleagues, all accustomed to the manufacture and maintenance of steam engines reliable enough for men's lives to depend on the pumps they powered. He had behind him both the money and the skills to assemble the package – engine, wheels, track – required to make steam locomotion an economic proposition.

Although Stephenson had built his first locomotive, the *Blucher* (named after the tough, rough Prussian general who was to save Wellington at Waterloo) as early as 1814, his first triumph was with the Stockton and Darlington Railway, opened to general amazement and acclaim in September 1825. This project was no Johnny-come-lately. It was first mooted in 1810, but two attempts were needed to get an enabling bill through Parliament, basically for a horse-powered way using not rails but plates to connect the coalmines around Bishop Auckland and Darlington. The day after the act received royal assent, one of its promoters, Edward Pease, a leading local Quaker banker (hence the S&D's nickname, the Quakers' line) received a visit from George

Stephenson, who persuaded him to resurvey the line with a view to using steam locomotion.

Within four years 25 miles (40km) of line had been built over rugged country, the longest and most ambitious 'way' of any description ever built in Britain, or indeed the world. Symbolically, it was the sun which provided the fire for the first run of *Locomotion*, the Stockton and Darlington's first locomotive. In the words of an old labourer present that day: 'Lantern and candle was to no use, so number 1 fire was put to her on line by the pour of the sun.' Thus, through accident rather than design, a direct link was established between the fire in heaven and a man-made flame which was to travel round the globe. The report of the inaugural run in the *Durham County Advertiser* three days later described the railway as a 'stupendous work . . . the longest railroad in the kingdom'. The event was witnessed by virtually the whole popula-

tion of the towns and villages along the route. The line was clearly seen as the precedent to a whole host of others. Toasts were drunk to the success of the Leeds and Hull Railway.

The Stockton and Darlington, the world's first public railway, did not involve much technical innovation, although Stephenson did use the malleable iron rails invented by a local engineer the previous year. These immediately replaced the existing and inadequate wrought-iron rails. Among other advantages the malleable iron rails could be 15ft (4.5m) long, thus greatly improving the smoothness of ride. But even the S&D did not have a monopoly: the owners had to permit other vehicles to run on their tracks – for the first few months, anyway. So, in theory, did shareholders in the Liverpool and Manchester. But it soon became clear that the operators needed to have total control over the trains as well as the tracks.

STEPHENSON'S "TRIUMPH,"

SIXTY MILES AN HOUR.

REGISTERED.

An excellent example of the hyperbole associated with early railways. It is extremely doubtful if any engine designed by either George or Robert Stephenson was capable of steaming for more than a few minutes at 60mph.

From its opening the Stockton and Darlington was a huge success, although it took all the ingenuity of Timothy Hackworth, the engineer responsible for the day-to-day running of the line, to improve the often inadequate performance of *Locomotion* and its three fellow locomotives. It attracted not only passengers by their thousands, but also coal by the hundreds of thousands of tons. A local grandee, Mr Lambton, had done a deal with the S&D, whereby coal due to be sent onwards by ship would pay only the apparently ruinously low rate of a halfpenny per ton per mile, an eighth of the price charged if the coal was to be used locally. Yet the low rate provided the new means of transport with the chance it needed to demonstrate its economic potential. It was soon carrying half a million tons of coal annually, fifty times the anticipated figure.

Although numerous schemes were planned over the next few years, some of which (including the cable-drawn Canterbury and Whitstable 'railway') actually came to fruition, the next landmark event was the rail connection established between Liverpool and Manchester in 1830. The opportunity was triggered by the abuse by the Bridgewater Canal Company of its monopoly of traffic between what were then the two biggest towns in Britain outside London, growing fast thanks to the cotton imported through Liverpool and transformed into cloth in Manchester. This scheme, originally proposed by William James, freed railways from their previous automatic connection with mining. It was also an indication that railways could compete successfully with the canals, which were then, it has to be remembered, an up-to-date means of transport, most of them having been built in the previous half-century.

For George Stephenson, the Liverpool and Manchester Railway was a nightmare that turned into glory. In his son's absence (Robert was by now in South America) George's limitations were exposed during Parliamentary hearings debating the vague and unsatisfactory survey he had conducted of the route. Despite this setback, he demonstrated the confidence and common sense which elevated railway engineers to innovators in civil as well as mechanical engineering when he tackled Chat Moss, the much-dreaded marsh between the two cities. Orthodox drainage ditches simply filled with water, but Stephenson showed that railways would be able to overcome natural obstacles hitherto deemed impassable. In L. T. C. Rolt's words: 'Stephenson's plan of floating his railway embankment across the Moss on a raft of brushwood and heather was put into operation. A vast tonnage of spoil was tipped only to be swallowed up, but Stephenson never lost heart and gradually a firm causeway began to stretch out into the Moss to confound the sceptics.'[6]

It was Robert, newly returned to England, who decisively settled the arguments between the advocates of fixed engines and supporters of locomotives. Richard Trevithick had shown that the power of a locomotive could be greatly increased by diverting the exhaust steam into a specially narrowed chimney. In the late 1820s, both Henry Booth, the treasurer of the Liverpool and Manchester, and the French engineer Marc Seguin suggested that the two tubes in the boiler should be replaced with a multiplicity of smaller ones, to draw hot gases from a separate fire box and so greatly increase the heating surface. At last they had solved the steam-raising problem and ensured that the locomotive would be capable of a sustained power output over long distances. It was Robert who put these ideas into operation with a quick succession of improved engines featuring ever-increasing numbers of tubes in their boilers.

As a result of the partnership between father and son, the modern world was conceived on 8 October 1829 during the trials held at Rainhill to decide how the trains on the Liverpool and Manchester would be powered. Robert Stephenson's *Rocket* attained a steady 29mph (46.7kph) on its later runs, proving that his design was far more reliable than the competing locomotives. These included not only other engines from Northumbria, but also some from the London-based manufacturers of road steam carriages, who had been the favourites. Rainhill symbolized the emancipation of steam power from the roads, which deprived roads of their hopes of carrying a mechanically advanced form of transport for three quarters of a century.

According to the original caption to this 19th-century print, 'the hind part' of this steam coach, designed by the improbably-named Mr Goldsworthy Gurney, contained 'the machinery for producing steam on a novel and secure principle'. Travelling at up to 10mph and carrying a mere six passengers inside and twelve outside, steam carriages like this designed to run on roads were no match for George Stephenson's railway engines.

In the year between the trials and the opening of the railway itself, George Stephenson garnered a great deal of (mostly favourable) publicity by driving specially honoured visitors along the completed sections of the line. The influential man-about-town Thomas Creevey was scared stiff. At 20mph (32kph) 'the quickest motion is to me frightful; it is really flying and it is impossible to divest yourself of the notion of instant death to all upon the least accident happening. It gave me a headache which has not left me yet.' But Creevey had to admit that even at 23mph (37kph) they were travelling 'with the same ease as to motion or absence of friction as the other reduced pace'. The passengers were comparing travel in the four-wheeled unsprung carts used as carriages with even rattlier coaches. Moreover, Creevey, and the equally frightened Lord Sefton, were clearly in the minority. 'He and I seem more struck with apprehension than the others.'

On 15 September 1830, the Liverpool and Manchester Railway was officially opened. Amid scenes of amazing media hype, farce and tragedy, eight special trains carried 600 important guests between the two cities. These included the Tory prime minister, the much-hated Duke of Wellington, who had to be protected from the mobs which swarmed all over the tracks. He was so scared that it took considerable persuasion to get him to complete the journey to Manchester. Another guest was the outspoken Tory

Christ Church and a 'coal staith' in Leeds. By 1829 steam locomotives were carrying loaded coal waggons in many places in the north of England.

A breakthrough in locomotive design. George Stephenson's *Northumbrian* was the first engine to be built with an integral firebox.

reformer William Huskisson, MP for Liverpool, friend of the city's merchants and an influential backer of the scheme. During the ceremonies, Huskisson, a notoriously clumsy individual, stepped into the path of a train and was killed in the world's first and most publicized railway accident, which also nearly claimed the life of the Austrian ambassador, Prince Esterhazy.

Rainhill had reinforced the idea of technological obsolescence. The railways were now replacing the canals built in the previous half-century and even the more modern system of post coaches running over macadamized road surfaces, which had represented the biggest advance in road transport since the Romans left Britain fourteen centuries earlier. Travelling time between major British cities had been halved between 1770 and 1830.

The locomotives soon assumed their modern form. By the end of 1830 the *Rocket* had been replaced by *Northumbrian*, another of Robert Stephenson's designs. 'In

northern ruggedness' so beloved, then as now, by effete
southerners. And no conquest was more useful, in public-
relations terms, anyway, than that of Fanny Kemble. She was
a pretty, witty member of the most distinguished theatrical
family in London, and was herself received, in the contem-
porary phrase, in the highest society. Naturally, Stephenson
was at his most charming when she climbed on to the footplate of the *Rocket*. They were both equally smitten.

We were introduced to the little engine which was to
drag us along the rails. She (for they make these
curious little fire horses all mares) consisted of a boiler,
a stove, a small platform, a bench, and behind the
bench a barrel containing enough water to prevent her
being thirsty for fifteen miles [24km] – the whole
machine not bigger than a common fire engine.
     . . . This snorting little animal, which I felt rather
inclined to pat, was then harnessed to our carriage,
and, Mr Stephenson having taken me on the bench of
the engine with him, we started at about ten miles an
hour. The steam horse being ill-adapted for going up
and downhill, the road was kept at a certain level, and
appeared sometimes to sink below the surface of the
earth and sometimes to rise above it. Almost at starting
it was cut through the solid rock, which formed a wall
on either side of it, about sixty feet high. You can't
imagine how strange it seemed to be journeying on
thus, without any visible cause of progress other than
the magical machine, with its flying white breath and
rhythmical, unvarying pace, between these rocky walls,
which are already clothed with moss and ferns and
grasses; and when I reflected that these great masses of
stone had been cut asunder to allow our passage thus
far below the surface of the earth, I felt as if no fairy
tale was ever half so wonderful as what I saw. Bridges
were thrown from side to side across the top of these
cliffs, and the people looking down upon us from them
seemed like pygmies standing in the sky.

all essential particulars,' wrote L. T. C. Rolt, 'the boiler of
the *Northumbrian* was the same as that fitted to every orthodox locomotive from that day to this.' Within a few years the
immortal *Rocket* had been relegated to the sidings. But it
had served its purpose: it had seen off the opposition and
proved that a mobile steam locomotive could replace not
only horsepower but also the stationary engines that everyone had assumed would be needed to conquer even the
slightest gradients.

George Stephenson's success was founded on more than
his technical capacities, reinforced by his son's more formal
engineering designs. One of his biggest contributions had
been as a propagandist. He exploited to the full the 'honest

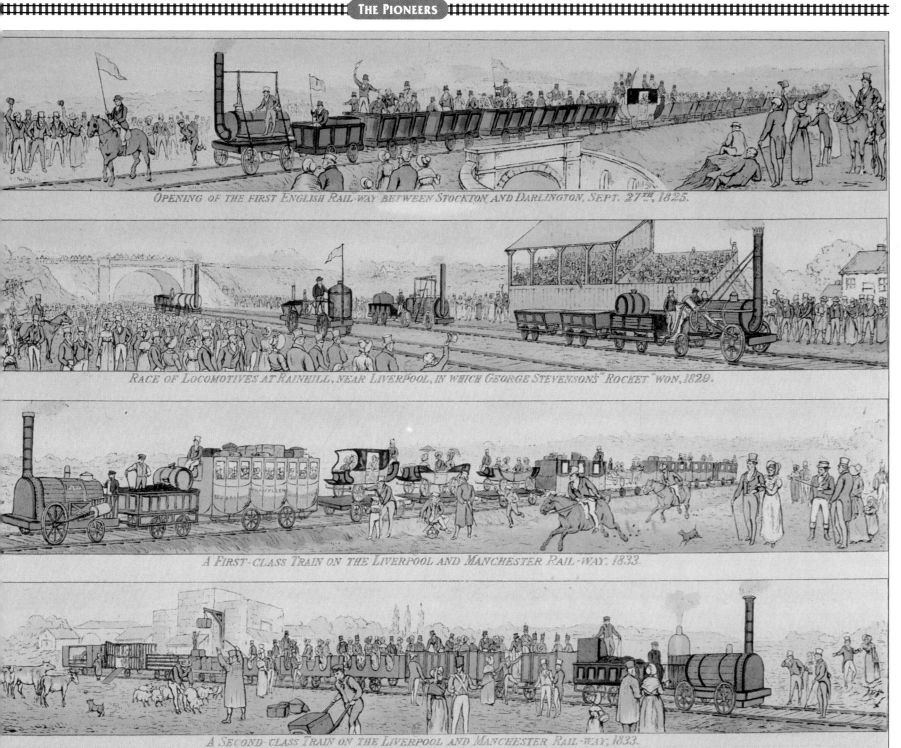

OPENING OF THE FIRST ENGLISH RAIL-WAY BETWEEN STOCKTON AND DARLINGTON, SEPT. 27TH, 1825.

RACE OF LOCOMOTIVES AT RAINHILL, NEAR LIVERPOOL, IN WHICH GEORGE STEVENSON'S "ROCKET" WON, 1829.

A FIRST-CLASS TRAIN ON THE LIVERPOOL AND MANCHESTER RAIL-WAY, 1833.

A SECOND-CLASS TRAIN ON THE LIVERPOOL AND MANCHESTER RAIL-WAY, 1833.

. . . After proceeding through this rocky defile, we presently found ourselves raised upon embankments ten or twelve feet [3–3.65m] high; we then came to a moss, or swamp, of considerable extent, on which no human foot could tread without sinking, and yet it bore the road which bore us.

. . . The engine having received its supply of water, the carriage was placed behind it, for it cannot turn, and was set off at its utmost speed, thirty-five miles an hour, swifter than a bird flies (for they tried the experiment with a snipe). You cannot conceive what the sensation of cutting the air was; the motion is as smooth as possible, too. I could either have read or written; and as it was, I stood up and with my bonnet off 'drank the air before me'. The wind, which was strong, or perhaps the force of our own thrusting against it, absolutely weighed my eyelids down . . . when I closed my eyes this sensation of flying was quite delightful and strange beyond description; yet strange as it was, I had a perfect sense of security, and not the slightest fear.

Part of the security clearly came from 'the master of all these marvels', George Stephenson, with whom Kemble confessed to being 'most horribly in love'.

There was once a man, who was born at Newcastle-upon-Tyne, who was a common coal-digger; this man had an immense constructiveness, which displayed itself in pulling his watch to pieces and putting it together again; in making a pair of shoes when he happened to be some days without occupation . . . He is a man of from fifty to fifty-five years of age; his face is fine, though careworn, and bears an expression of deep thoughtfulness; his mode of explaining his ideas is peculiar and very original, striking and forcible; and

although his accent indicates strongly his north-country birth, his language has not the slightest touch of vulgarity or coarseness . . . A common sheet of paper is enough for love, but a foolscap can alone contain a railroad and my ecstasies . . . He has certainly turned my head.

Fanny Kemble was not alone, and not only in Britain, but also around the rest of the world. For Stephenson was, justifiably, always confident that, as he told a devout Methodist friend, 'I will send the locomotive as the great missionary over the world.'

The favourite which fell, or rather broke down. *Novelty*, **hotly-tipped to win the trials at Rainhill. However, in the event, the trials confirmed the superiority of George Stephenson's designs.**

CHAPTER FOUR

THE MIRACULOUS DECADES

THE IMMEDIATE SUCCESS of the Liverpool and Manchester Railway sent shock waves throughout Britain, and then more slowly, outwards around the world. By 1833 a 'railway companion' describing an excursion along the line was justified in claiming that 'already locomotive power is rapidly superseding every other species of conveyance throughout the civilized world'. In the fourth decade of the nineteenth century, British engineers proved that railways could be built through the most inhospitable terrain; that the resulting lines could be highly profitable for the promoters and could benefit the towns and landowners along their route. Railways were becoming the most important symbol of the industrial, economic and financial strength of the age, the image of men's dreams of power, wealth and glory. It was equally clear that they would also bear the inescapable burden of financial malversation and generally inept government interference.

By 1835 forty-one different railway companies (not including horsepowered routes) had been authorized by Parliament to build 970 miles (1,561km) of railway, of which 338 (544km) had already been completed. In 1836 a further fifty-seven railway bills were presented to Parliament, and the thirty-five that became law provided for another 955 miles (1,537km) of line.

By the end of the decade passengers were able to travel by train over 200 miles (322km) north from the new station at Euston to Preston on a system that embraced Birmingham, Manchester and Liverpool, the country's three largest cities. By the end of the 1840s they could get from London to Edinburgh and Glasgow by train in twelve hours or less, and by 1852, with the completion of what is now the East Coast Main Line from London to Newcastle, most of the country's mainline network had been built. Already all the physical paraphernalia we associate with rail travel – the stations, the tunnels, the embankments, the signals – had assumed the form they were to retain to the present day.

By the time the London and Birmingham Railway opened in 1839, the public was so used to railways that there were vociferous complaints when passengers were ferried by coach (at the previously respectable speed of 11mph [17.7kph]) over a stretch of line not completed for several months because of difficulties in constructing the Kilsby Tunnel. The public's astonishingly speedy acceptance of this fearsome new form of transport was largely due to its excellent safety record. There were only two deaths among the 5 million or so passengers carried by the Liverpool and Manchester in its first ten years of operation.

The enthusiasm of Charles Greville, the clerk to the Privy Council, was doubtless echoed by many less exalted passengers. In 1837 he decided, on an impulse, to 'run down' by train to see the Earl of Derby. He was delighted. 'The first sensation,' he wrote, 'is a slight degree of nervousness and a feeling of being run away with, but a sense of security soon supervenes . . . it entirely renders all other travelling irksome

The dangers of building railway lines too close to a turbulent sea: the results of a landslip in 1852 near the quaintly-named Parson and Clerk Rock on the south Devon coast.

Robert Stephenson, the brilliant son of a brilliant father. Unlike George, Robert was an equally effective civil and mechanical engineer.

and tedious by comparison.' The next year he records how, when summoned by Queen Victoria, as a matter of course he took the train to Slough and then walked from the station to Windsor Castle.

The Liverpool and Manchester spawned a rat race of previously unimaginable pace. According to John Francis, 'Men talk of "getting up the steam", of "railway speed" and reckon distances by hours and minutes. The story of a gentleman who left Manchester in the morning, who went thence to Liverpool, purchased and took back with him 150 tons of cotton, and having sold it, returned to Liverpool on a similar errand with similar success, was a stereotyped story for the press.'[1]

At a more humble level, the Manchester weavers found they could use the railway to save time on deliveries by taking it in turns to carry packages for each other. But, as Francis avers, 'railway managers are political economists', and for a time they allowed each passenger to carry only a single pack. The weavers responded by boycotting the line, and won their point – the first recorded instance of a populist revolt against excessive charges or unreasonable regulations imposed by the almighty, monopolistic railway.

Railway histories have, traditionally, made much of the opposition mounted by the landowning aristocracy, who often made life a misery for the promoters when the House of Lords committees examined railway bills. Their opposition was not, in itself, surprising. They had a vested interest in the success of the turnpikes, because their fields grew the fodder required by the horses. A few landowners objected on principle, but most were practical men. They did not want their hunting and shooting interfered with or their views spoiled; they were appalled at the behaviour of the promoters and their surveyors. However, they were greedy, and soon found that opposition could be astonishingly profitable as towns grew, or were even created by, the railways. As Francis puts it, 'Houses grew in the place of corn, and . . . ground rents more than compensated for grain.'

At first the upper classes kept their distance by travelling in their own carriages. 'To enable private carriages to travel

along the railway,' wrote a 'tourist', 'flat forms are provided, upon which the carriage is raised and its wheels firmly secured upon the platforms by moveable grooves.' But these were uncomfortable and inconvenient, and by the end of the decade the gentry travelled like everyone else. By 1840 the first special royal coach had been built for the Dowager Queen Adelaide. Prince Albert, that apostle of modernity, was predictably an early enthusiast, and soon converted his wife. In 1842 Queen Victoria noted how she had come to London 'by the railroad from Windsor, in half an hour, free from the dust and crowd and heat, and I am quite charmed with it'.

Of the early lines, the most significant was that built by Robert Stephenson between London and Birmingham. Not only was this the first and crucial link between the capital and a major provincial city (and, indirectly, between the capital, Liverpool and Manchester as well), but the new railway also ran parallel with, and often very close to, the country's foremost man-made waterway, the Grand Junction Canal, whose twenty-six speedy daily flyboats carried urgent goods, and Watling Street, where sixteen coaches ran every day between the two cities. With the London and Birmingham, the newly omnipotent – and private – railway interest had dealt a deadly blow to the public, communal thoroughfares, canal and road, where the small man could compete on equal terms with major carriers. The line presented a formidable challenge because the Stephensons had chosen the most direct route, ignoring tempting – and flatter – alternatives via Oxford, High Wycombe and Banbury. They kept the ruling gradient to a mere 1:330 through rolling countryside by incorporating cuttings and tunnels of an unprecedented depth and length. The level track Robert Stephenson demanded involved earthworks of a size not required by even the most ambitious canals – as did the broad swathe cut through the countryside by Isambard Kingdom Brunel's Great Western on its way from London to Bristol a few years later.

But it was the London to Brighton line, opened in 1841, which finally proved that the railway could conquer even the most efficient stagecoach service. The coaches to Brighton ran every hour, covering the 56 miles (90km) to London in under five hours, yet within a couple of years they had become relics of a bygone age. With the post coaches went the dependent

One of John Bourne's evocative prints from 1837 of the massive earthworks required to build the railway from London to Birmingham.

businesses – coaching inns, the ostlers and the carters – some of them substantial. Only a few of the owners managed to switch trades, most famously William James Chaplin, who sold his concern and invested the proceeds in the London and Southampton Railway, of which he became chairman.

Surprisingly, the locomotives changed less than any other aspect of rail travel, although boiler pressures were steadily increased, thanks to more durable iron and the great improvement in valve gears. By the end of the 1840s most freight engines were being built on the 0–6–0 principle, with six driving wheels for maximum adhesion, a configuration combined

with inside frames and rear wheels mounted to the rear of the fire box. By contrast, the locomotives for passenger trains employed a variety of configurations, many (including those for Brunel's fastest expresses) with only two driving wheels.

In the 1830s two great engineers improved on the Stephensons' ideas. George's former pupil Joseph Locke refused to accept that lines had to be more or less level because of the relatively low power of the engines, arguing that locomotive power would increase sufficiently to cope with reasonably steep gradients. To put this theory into practice, Locke found a much shorter, though steeper, alternative

Another Bourne print showing how even the 'Engine Houses' on the London to Birmingham line were graced with crenallations.

How curiously quaint the Liverpool and Manchester Railway is made to appear, and how easily travellers could compare the engines with horses – if only because they both needed regular drinks of water.

to the lengthy coastal route proposed by the Stephensons to the west of the Lake District for the route between Preston and Carlisle, and on to Glasgow. Locke was proved right, but it was another 150 years before the French used the virtually unlimited power available from electric traction to construct new ultra-fast lines with gradients far steeper than Locke or any of his successors had dared envisage for anything other than mountain railways.

A much more fundamental challenge was mounted by Isambard Kingdom Brunel. 'Looking at the speeds which I contemplated would be adopted on railways and the masses to be moved,' he later told a government committee, 'it seemed to me that the whole machine was too small for the work to be done, and that it required that the parts should be on a scale more commensurate with the mass and the velocity to be attained.' But by 1835, when he proposed his alternative – and technically superior – 7ft (2,134mm) gauge, it was already too late for him to hope to change the course of history. Although broad-gauge trains ran on

Brunel's Great Western until 1892, the fate of the 7ft gauge had been sealed half a century earlier. In western Europe, once the Belgians, the pioneers in railway-building outside Britain, had adopted the Stephenson gauge, their neighbours were eventually obliged to follow suit. Even so, railways in continental Europe were built to allow broader, taller trains, wagons and coaches than most British lines.

Nonetheless, Brunel did have a considerable influence. Thanks to the superb level track he laid down, his broad-gauge system set incredible standards of speed. By the mid 1840s his trains to Bristol were averaging over 40mph (64kph). His conspicuous success put the advocates of the normal narrow gauge on their mettle. As a result most of the major towns in the country were linked by trains averaging over 30mph (48kph) by the end of the 1840s – trains developed far faster than later forms of transport like the motor vehicle and the aeroplane. (Incidentally, it was Brunel who set up the first railway town at Swindon, then a mere village at the point where engines were changed.)

The pressures of the 1830s dealt a final blow to the idea of the 'renaissance engineer', capable of designing an engine or a railway line at will, and the successors of the Stephensons and Brunel rarely combined civil and mechanical engineering work. George Stephenson was eager to have as much power as possible; indeed, he attempted to extend his monopoly to include not only the surveying, engineering, construction and operation of the railway, but also the building of the locomotives. By contrast, although Robert Stephenson's original contribution had been as a mechanical engineer, in the 1830s and 1840s he was forced to concentrate on his civil work. And Brunel's interference in locomotive design often had rather unhappy results.

So by the 1850s, the engineers' profession had been divided. The civil engineers were now responsible for the infrastructure and the tracks, and the mechanicals for the engines, the trains and the signalling. Specialization was soon carried through to the whole process of railway construction and operation. Railways were initiated by 'projectors', more or less honest financial entrepreneurs; the proposals were promoted in Parliament by lobbyists, financed through brokers and bankers in the City of London and carried through on the orders of contractors. The engineers had quickly learned that it was useless to rely on a horde of small subcontractors for such vast projects, so they gave contracts to men like Thomas Brassey – who acquired a totally deserved reputation, thanks to his unusual honesty and extraordinary organizing capacity – and Samuel Morton Peto, the models for the contractors who erupted across the globe in the succeeding decades.

These contractors were a special breed. The world's railway networks were built both because of and despite them. Their energies and their boldness were matched only by their frequent dishonesty. The first generation, at least, were not mere builders – they were part shysters, part entrepreneurs, part financiers, part civil engineers, wholly typical of an age that bred chancers of every description. They were a transitory group, loners, one-offs who did not found great enterprises; a group that took advantage of unrepeatable opportunities to exploit their peculiar talents of organization and financial daring.

Another breed not destined to last longer than the construction period were the navigators or 'navvies', whose name was coined during the building of Britain's canal system in the generation before the arrival of the railways. The chaos created by these 'armies of steam' has never been better captured than by Charles Dickens in his celebrated description of the construction of the line into Euston in *Dombey and Son*.

The first shock of a great earthquake had . . . rent the whole neighbourhood to its centre. Traces of its course were visible on every side. Houses were knocked down; streets broken through and stopped; deep pits and trenches dug in the ground; enormous heaps of earth and clay thrown up; buildings that were undermined and shaking, propped by great beams of wood . . . Everywhere were bridges that led nowhere; thoroughfares that were wholly impassable; Babel towers of chimneys, wanting half their height; temporary

Left: **The cartoonists of the 1830s had a field-day at the way they – and everyone else – assumed that the newfangled railways would disturb the animal kingdom and would ruin the economy of the horse-drawn traffic on Britain's post roads.**

Opposite: **A careworn Isambard Kingdom Brunel, the genius behind the broad-gauge Great Western Railway in a photograph which shows signs of the overwork which killed him in his early fifties.**

By the early 1840s, impressive viaducts, like this one on the line between Brighton and Lewes, were relatively commonplace.

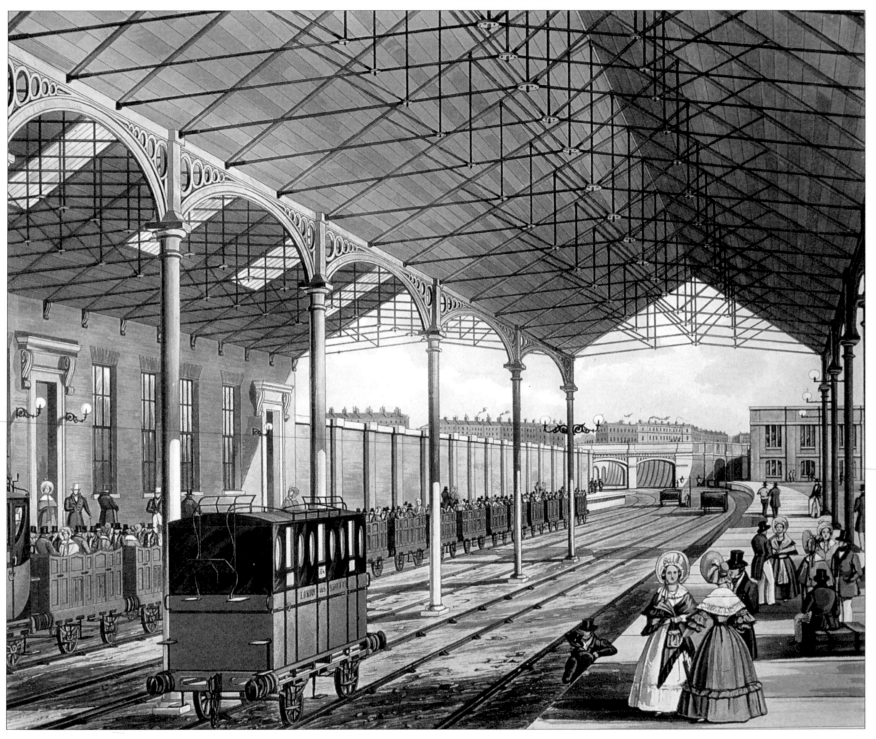

wooden houses and enclosures, in the most unlikely situations; carcases of ragged tenements and fragments of unfinished walls and arches, and piles of scaffolding, and wildernesses of bricks, and giant forms of cranes, and tripods straddling above nothing.

This massive disruption of the urban landscape left a permanent cavern, to the side of which now stands Gloucester Crescent, which boasts some of the trendiest accommodation in London, much favoured by the capital's celebrated intellectuals.

The spread of the railways forced towns and cities to react to the intrusion. Liverpool's response was positive: its council was prepared to invest in a tunnel, costing well over £100,000 ($150,000) from Edgehill to Lime Street in the centre of the city. As a result Liverpool became by far the biggest English city to have a single, central station. By contrast, Manchester had three disconnected termini; so, originally, did Birmingham, where the first terminus of the first major line to link a capital with a major provincial city was on the edge of the urban area. And the worthies of another historic city, York, were so keen that, as Gordon Biddle relates, they 'positively welcomed one inside the medieval walls that required an arch cutting through the fabric . . . the station covered the known sites of three Roman baths'.[2]

The stations themselves quickly assumed their permanent character. During the 1830s architects used a variety of styles to glorify the new form of transport. The most astonishing was at Euston, where in the mid-1840s Philip Hardwicke built a magnificent classical great hall. A grand staircase led to the equally grand offices of the directors of the London and North-Western Railway, the largest railway company and the biggest enterprise in the land, and the prototype of the arrogant, self-sufficient, lordly railway firm. The splendour of Euston was echoed at the other end of the line, where Birmingham's first station boasted an Ionic portico, the Midlands' equivalent of the triumphal arch at Euston. Both Euston and Birmingham offered another convenience: a station hotel. On 18 September 1838, *The Times* reported that

'part of the magnificent station house in Birmingham has recently been licensed as an hotel . . . so that passengers, if they think proper, may be accommodated with every good thing without leaving the company's premises'.

These schemes required the investment of more capital more quickly than any previous such enterprise, yet at first, at least, it was easy to raise the money. Until the mid-1840s no one really believed that any railway could be unprofitable. In the dry words of a modern economic historian, 'Private capital was forthcoming for railway investment in the late 1830s and early 1840s only because the eventual lowness of the private rate of return on some projects was not anticipated.'[3] And Henry Grote Lewin explained: 'The spirit of unreasoning optimism was in the air; the possibilities and advantages which the country was to attain with liberal railway communication were deemed to be boundless.'[4] But even this golden age of innocence was full of dubious schemes, each promoted in a separate bill which provided opportunities for much debate and more bribery. The sums involved were gigantic: Thomas Brassey built 60 miles of difficult line in northern Italy for the same cost – £430,000 ($645,000) – as it took to put through the bill for a single English railway, the Lancashire and Yorkshire.

From the beginning the railways' profits created envy, inevitably expressed in demands for government control. This was somewhat unfair. John Francis reports: 'It was said, and with much justice, that railways were as beneficial as canals, but that, though the latter averaged 33 per cent, there had been no restriction on their dividends, no claim on their profits.'[5] By the early 1840s politicians were already heavily involved. Lord Dalhousie, who carried his enthusiasm for railways and for government control over them to India when he became governor-general, even suggested that the government should be given the power to nationalize the railways if their profits were found to be excessive over a ten-year period. His idea was that even before a railway could be built a board would examine the promoters' capacities and their forecasts of costs, revenues and profits. In the event these ideas were swept away and the railway

The first rather primitive station at Euston Square in 1837. Two years later this temporary structure was replaced by Philip Hardwick's masterpiece, the first station in the world to celebrate railways in all their glory.

interest prevailed, provoking the complaint that 'in our country alone has the right of possession in perpetuity been granted by the government'.

Not surprisingly, earlier 'canal manias' were soon eclipsed by the railway boom which erupted in 1845. This was a result not only of the increasing success of the railways, but also of the influence of the speculators in the City of London. Initially, the money had not come principally from London. According to Francis, 'The London merchants had doubted the practicability of the iron way; they had derided the notion of the locomotive; they had scarcely even adventured in the shares.'[6] The heart of the matter was in Liverpool, where throughout the 1830s speculation reaped great rewards. But with the increasing proliferation of lines into and around London, the city became involved. The press whipped up the excitement: the line from London to Exeter was proposed partly because 'it was nearly the road adopted by the Romans'. Were not 'railways the emblems of internal confidence and prosperity . . . the great levellers, bringing the producer and consumer into immediate contact? By railways the whole country may be, and will be, under the blessing of divine providence, cultivated as a garden.'

In 1845 Parliament passed 225 bills, and a further 270 in the following session. In all, they provided for 4,540 miles (7,306km) of track which were to cost £100 million ($150 million) – well over £10 billion ($15 billion) in today's terms. Members were not exactly impartial: in 1845, the names of 157 of them were on the registers of new railway companies, and one MP boasted of being able to command 100 votes. Titled personages were naturally much sought after by promoters (one man was a director of twenty-three companies, and another of twenty-two).

The investment mania was not confined to the fat cats. In a Yorkshire vicarage Emily and Anne Brontë ignored the warnings of their sister Charlotte and invested their meagre savings in the Yorkshire and Midland Railway. In London, 'men were pointed out in the streets who had made their tens of thousands. [Sober citizens] saw the whole world railway mad

. . . they entered the whirlpool and were carried away by the vortex . . . their infant daughters were large subscribers; their youthful sons were down for thousands. Like drunken men they lost their caution and gave their signatures for everything that was offered.' Even Charles Greville dabbled, although he had been warned against it by the governor of the Bank of England, who 'never remembered in all his experience anything like the present speculation . . . and that there could not fail to be a fearful reaction'.

The subsequent panic was, naturally, blamed on the railway promoters, although Lewin points to the general economic situation: the failure of the Irish potato crop and the famine which followed; the repeal of the Corn Laws, the subsequent sharp reduction in the price of grain, and the consequent severe shortage of spare capital for investment were all factors.

The boom, and the crash, were epitomized by the fortunes of the man aptly nicknamed the 'Railway King'. MP George Hudson, the all-but-crowned king of his native York, was the very archetype of the vulgar, swaggering adventurer bred worldwide by the railways. In the words of his biographer, 'his energies flowed into four distinct channels: first,

Left: **One of the massive engines designed by Brunel's long-suffering designer, Daniel Gooch, for use on the GWR.**

Opposite: **In 1870 express locomotives were still being designed with single driving wheels. This 'Stirling Single', with its massive 8-foot diameter driving wheels, thundered over the** *Great Northern's* **tracks until it was withdrawn from service as late as 1907.**

railway, dock and other industrial enterprises; secondly, banking and finance; thirdly, the acquisition and management of landed property; lastly, politics local and national.' At the height of his powers he controlled 'a vast network of enterprises such as no one man before his time had dared to try and combine'.[7]

Nevertheless, all his activities centred on the railways – proof, if any were needed, that the new transport system was the epicentre of all political and economic activity in the two decades after 1830. To the majority who fawned on Hudson, 'he was as a mountebank upon a platform at a fair – one who could draw money from their pockets by tricks which kept them perpetually gaping', says Lambert. He had the nerve and the bulldozing drive to push through the required bills and amalgamations; to dismiss rebellious workers and run a miserably inadequate service without them; to act as the spokesman of the whole railway interest in watering down Gladstone's original proposals for controlling them in a private deal with the country's most principled and intelligent statesman.

At the height of his fame Hudson was almost literally worshipped. His grand mansion in Kensington was besieged by the great and good; his every move an object of wonder. His basic aim, as he told a House of Commons committee, was a controlled monopoly to be achieved through a mixture of amalgamations, leases and purchases. Yet although at the height of his power he controlled 1,450 (2,334km) of the 5,000 miles (8,047km) of railway in Britain, those lines never formed a natural system. His fate was inevitable once his enemies had managed to promote a direct line from London to York, thus greatly reducing the value of the tangled routes he controlled.

Hudson perfected most of the fraudulent devices later employed by company promoters the world over. He manipulated the stocks of the many firms in which he had an interest; he sold land from his own estate to his own railways; he bought rails and other equipment cheaply and sold it at a higher price to his railways, and withheld the money he owed to landowners and contractors.

His downfall was sparked off by a crisis in the affairs of the Eastern Counties Railway. The chairman of the investigating committee was a Quaker, which added moral and linguistic force to his interrogation – 'Didst thou, after the accountant had made up the yearly accounts, alter any of the figures? . . . Wilt thou give the committee an answer, yea or nay?' As *The Times* observed later, 'Mr Hudson's position was not only new in itself, but absolutely a new thing in the world altogether. His subjects exalted him to the position of those early kings who knew no difference between their own purses and the public exchequer . . . His colleagues knew this, the shareholders knew it. They would have tolerated it to this day, without the smallest objection, but for the unlucky circumstance that Hudson had outlived their success.'

The promoters, however, were not deterred for long, and by the end of the century Britain was lumbered with an unnecessarily complex, overcompetitive railway system with countless, inevitably uncommercial branch lines, as each major system strove to squeeze every last possible drop of traffic from its hinterland. The development left the British public with an ambivalent view of its great achievement, the world's first railway system, together with a sceptical, if not downright hostile attitude towards railways, railway directors and railway companies that has lasted to this day.

George Hudson, the Railway King seen in all his glory. Before his empire collapsed in the late 1840s, this prototype of the sleazy city financier persuaded thousands of innocent investors to put their money into his – generally fraudulent – railway companies.

CHAPTER FIVE

SPEED IS THE ESSENCE

FROM THE BEGINNING railways have always been about speed. Their shape, their design, even the fact that steam-powered locomotives were intended to run primarily on rails rather than roads, were all decided by the Rainhill trials, where speed was the priority. It was not so much a question of the top speed reached by a train for a few miles on a favourable (and usually downhill) stretch of track – however much publicity that might attract – as of the capacity of a train to provide a regular fast service over long distances. Yet throughout railway history speeds have increased only in fits and starts since improvements have depended on new trains or awaited a complete reconstruction or electrification of a line.

The first speed record was set by George Stephenson when he reached 36mph (58kph) while carrying the dying body of William Huskisson to hospital. This was an exceptional run, as were many of the other records claimed over the next century and a half. Such landmarks included the first mile a minute (achieved by the GWR in 1845); the first time a locomotive reached 100mph (161kph) – again, recorded by the GWR, in 1904; the 126mph (203kph) clocked up by the steam engine *Mallard* in 1937, and the 133.5mph (215kph) attained by the diesel-powered *Flying Hamburger* a couple of years earlier. Today the world speed record is in the hands of the French, who have recorded 512kph (317mph) with a relatively standard TGV on ordinary tracks.

More significant were the average speeds achieved on regular services, though even these were usually reached by trains which were special, and therefore irregular and more expensive. Within two decades of the opening of the Stockton to Darlington line, in 1824, its trains were covering relatively long distances at an average of 40mph (64kph), four times the speed of a horse. In 1844, Daniel Gooch, Brunel's locomotive designer, drove the first train on the newly opened 193-mile (311-km) route from London to Exeter at an average speed of 41.4mph (67kph) and within a few years trains were regularly travelling the 53 miles (85km) from Didcot to Paddington at over a mile a minute, thanks to the broad-gauge tracks which provided much greater stability, and much more room for broader boilers, than the Stephenson gauge. Yet until the First World War few, if any, regular services anywhere in the world averaged more than 50mph (80kph). The time required to travel the 120 miles (193km) between London and Bristol was a mere two hours 45 minutes by 1852. It took another fifty years to reduce the time to two hours and seventy years to bring it down a further half-hour.

By their very nature, railways tend not to be directly competitive, so there have been only a few 'races' between different railway companies. In the United States the prime 800-mile (1,287-km) route between New York and Chicago was the scene of one such battle. The British equivalent, admittedly over a distance of only 500 miles (805km), between London and Scotland, was the setting for two others, in the 1890s and 1930s respectively. The first, the so-called Great Railway Race of 1895, has been described by C. David Wilson as a

As the name implies, the Intercity 225, built for the newly-electrified East Coast Main Line from London to Edinburgh, was designed to achieve 225kph (140mph). But because of signalling problems and drivers' objections it can only travel at 200kph (125mph).

'last hurrah', for this was the year that saw the first London Motor Exhibition.

The races were a showpiece of the whole industrial system the railways themselves had brought about. Wilson explains: 'The ability to race trains is predicated upon having a line to race on, locomotives and rolling stock to race with, and a team of managers, supervisors and workmen to put the order to race into practical existence. To achieve this situation requires a high degree of organization, substantial levels of investment, both of capital and labour, plus the desire and necessary authority to be able to carry such a proposition into being.' In practical terms this involved

> the nature and quality of the total route and its engineering standard . . . ruling gradients, track alignment, and the strength and quality of rail in use, the amount and severity of curves, the quality of signalling equipment and even track layouts at important stations and junctions . . . There are any number of pitfalls involved in conducting an event of the size of the races, not least of which is that element usually labelled 'human error'. The miles of track, the countless signals and signal boxes, stations, level crossings, coaches, couplings, engine changes, coal, water – the different possibilities for errors are incalculable, and they are all subject to the inherent vagaries of human agency.'[1]

Matching the performances of trains at over a mile a minute for over 500 miles (805km) would not have been possible without various elements of the new civilization, not just locomotives powerful enough to pull the trains (indeed, the locomotives used were not new: most were designs dating from the 1870s). What mattered more was the telegraph, without which the signalmen would not have known what was going on, and the many technical developments since Daniel Gooch's time. O. S. Nock adds:

> Not only were steel rails coming into general use, together with steel tyres, but much harder steels were being introduced. Running over such rails would have

The Royal Scot, one of the LMS's most glamorous locomotives – and trains – in 1934, before the streamliners came on the scene.

much less deflection than hitherto, and the resistance to motion would be less. Improvements were also being made in the quality of the road bed, with better ballasting and better drainage; these latter had been in progress over a longer period, and there can be little doubt that it was the quality of the rails themselves and of locomotive wheel tyres that made the greatest contribution.[2]

The first hint of competition began in early August 1869, to capture the interest of the many well-heeled travellers who would shortly be heading north from London for the opening of the grouse-shooting season. The North-Eastern Railway, with its Scottish partner the North British, inaugurated a night train which took a mere ten hours to cover the 400 miles (644km) from King's Cross to Edinburgh. However, it was not until the Forth Bridge opened in 1890 that the competition got going in earnest. The bridge gave a great advantage to the companies operating on the east coast, but, even earlier, by the time the first grouse were being shot in 1888, both consortia, one on the east, the other on the west-coast route, were running trains at an average of over 50mph (80kph) from London to Edinburgh.

By the early 1890s the Americans were running faster trains over an even longer distance, between New York and Buffalo, which set another challenge, but in Britain the participants were preoccupied with their own internal battle which came

King Charles II, one of the GWR's powerful (if heavy) King-class 4–6–0s, arriving at Bath from Swindon on Brunel's famous line from London to Bristol.

to a head in the summer of 1895. The word battle is no exaggeration. The Marquis of Tweedale, chairman of the North British, ordered his general manager to beat the west-coast consortium 'at any cost'. By this time the 1889 Railway Regulation Act had ensured that standards of braking and signalling, previously lamentably low, had greatly improved, boosting the confidence of everyone involved in running the trains. In addition, introduction of water troughs had enabled trains to run non-stop for far longer distances – including the 160-odd miles (257km) from Euston to Crewe, which was a great help to the London and North-Western, the dominant partner in the west-coast consortium. Even so the strain was appalling, on men as well as on locomotives. During the seven weeks of the 1895 race period, the extremely fast stretch from Crewe to Carlisle, generally run at over a mile a minute – the record was an average of 67mph (108kph), including the steep climb over Shap Summit – was operated in the main by two locomotives and four crews.

The two sides were not really batting on a level pitch. The east-coast route was slightly shorter and less hilly. On the minus side, though, the last section to Aberdeen included a single-line stretch, which meant that the train had to slow down to under 30mph (48kph) to receive the 'token' which ensured that there was no other train on that particular piece of track. The west-coaster, meanwhile, faced a number of long climbs, notably that over Beattock Summit, made famous even to non-railway lovers by the phrase in W. H. Auden's poem, 'Night Mail': 'Pulling up Beattock, a steady climb – the gradient's against her but she's on time.'

The races were triggered off by the decision by the North-Eastern to 'accelerate' the 8pm departure on 1 July 1895. The London and North-Western countered a fortnight later and boasted of its achievements in a huge poster campaign. The battle attracted enormous public interest, commanding regular newspaper reports and drawing crowds even in the middle of the night to cheer on the racers (the race involved night trains, which made matters much easier for the participants since there were fewer other trains to be shunted aside). Excitement grew as the times of arrival in Aberdeen got ear-

lier and earlier (although there was a slight hiatus in the first fortnight of August while the companies struggled to transport the aristocratic crowds anxious to get at the grouse).

The last spasm of the race saw some considerable achievements, including a reduction of one and a quarter hours in a mere six weeks in the journey time between London and Carlisle. The most impressive feat of the whole competition was the consistency of the London and North-Western. The time it set for the London to Aberdeen route, 540 miles (869km) in 512 minutes, remained a record for steam power until diesels came along – and even today the best time, and that on the east-coast run, is 430 minutes. But the strain proved too much, and before the end of August both sides withdrew from the race, both claiming victory, but both fearful of taking further risks.

In retrospect the race appeared rather pointless. As the London and North-Western's line superintendent pointed out at the time, 'There was really nothing gained by the arrival at 6.25 or 6.30 in Aberdeen. The hotels were not open for their regular work; the discomfort of unprepared breakfast tables, or the accompaniment of dusting damsels in the coffee rooms, were travellers' annoyances rather than conveniences. The hour earlier into Aberdeen was a drawback rather than a benefit.'[3]

The tacit and unsigned truce agreed in 1895 lasted until the early 1930s, Inevitably, in the interim, other companies, most obviously the Great Western, which benefited from Brunel's broad racetrack from London to Bristol, were anxious to show what they were capable of. Opportunities arose occasionally with royal trains (notably those carrying King Edward VII, who liked his trains as fast as his ladies) or where there was competition. Indeed, the first train to 'do the ton' was the GWR's *City of Truro*, in the course of a race in 1904 between the GWR and the London and South-Western to convey passengers and mail to London from liners which had docked at Plymouth – although there was some dispute among enthusiasts, then known as 'railwayacs', as to whether the *City of Truro* did in fact reach the speed of 104mph (167kph) later claimed for the run.

Opposite: **The *Flying Scotsman* itself, headed by *Spearmint*, an engine named after a Derby winner, en route for Edinburgh on 9 July 1934.**

Below: **An historic occasion: the *Junior Scotsman* follows five minutes after its senior brother on the first non-stop run from King's Cross to Edinburgh on 20 July 1931.**

The GWR continued to set the pace for the next thirty years. The company's chief mechanical engineer, G. J. Churchward, unlike some of his more egotistical counterparts, simply built engines absorbing the best practice of all its rivals. The 4–6–0 engines he produced, the Castles and the heavier King class, were taken as models by the GWR's competitors. One of his opposite numbers, the ambitious Nigel Gresley of the LNER, absorbed the lessons into his 4–6–2 Pacific flyers.

The races of the 1930s were a reaction to the slump, a defiance of prevailing economic conditions. They were set off by the GWR, which ran what was described by disgusted rivals as a 'stunt train', the *Cheltenham Flyer*, a mid-afternoon special that eventually ran at the world-record average of 71mph (114kph), with long stretches at over 80mph (129kph).

Gresley, the key figure in these races, displayed an odd mixture of characteristics. As an innovator he had already introduced the more efficent 'buck-eye' couplings and articulated carriages with a single bogie supporting two coaches. But he was also something of a self-publicist, and thus interested not only in speed but also in the capacity of engines to run non-stop between London and Scotland. Hence the introduction of the 'corridor' tender, which enabled crews to be changed in mid-journey (this was something of a gimmick since in practice it saved only four and half minutes).

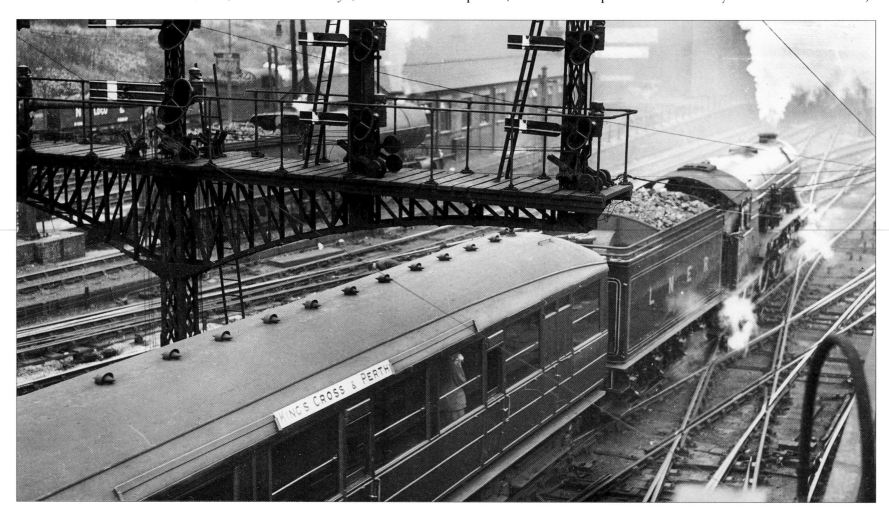

In 1928 the LNER's flagship train, the *Flying Scotsman*, started to run non-stop from London to Edinburgh. This was a truly special train, the acme of interwar luxury, with its special carriages for the ladies' hairdresser, the cinema and the cocktail bar. In 1935, when George V celebrated twenty-five years on the throne, the LNER added the *Silver Jubilee*. By then Gresley's first streamliner, *Silver Link*, had proved capable of running for over 43 miles (69km), a world record, at over 100mph (161kph).

But it was the accession of George VI to the throne following Edward VIII's abdication in December 1936 that started off the real rivalry. In 1933, William Stanier of the London Midland and Scottish had produced his first Pacific-type locomotive. He went on to design two others, the Princesses and the more powerful Princess Coronations, named in honour of the new king's daughters, the Princesses Elizabeth and Margaret. These locomotives powered the new express, which, continuing his theme, he named the *Coronation Scot*. It was designed to reach Glasgow from Euston in six hours and in 1939 its advertisements claimed an average speed of 61.7mph (99kph), a couple of miles an hour slower than achieved in 1895 – albeit with special trains. In June 1937 the train had set a world record 113mph (182kph) on a trial run for the press (though the train had to be braked more than sharply when it hit a 20mph (32kph) speed restriction on a curve at Crewe at 52mph [84kph]).

But the LNER was not to be outdone, and the competition culminated in the famous record speed of 126mph (203kph) set by Nigel Gresley's *Mallard*. The locomotive's streamlined shape has become familiar over the years, but the more important streamlining was inside the engines. It was the work of a famous French engineer, André Chapelon, in redesigning the steam passages, ports and passageways within the engine that made all the difference by allowing a free flow of steam. But once again the races imposed an appalling strain on the engines. On a previous record-breaking run, the big end of the cylinder in one engine completely disintegrated, as did the same overstressed component in the course of *Mallard*'s famous journey.

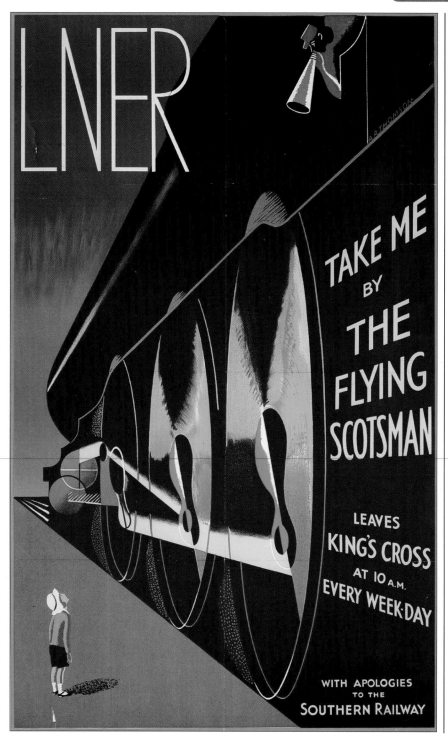

Every British schoolboy may still know the *Mallard*'s name and be able to quote its record speed, but its fame is, to me, a demonstration of British insularity. As one of the few far-sighted railwaymen of the postwar years put it: 'In the teeth of those who will not hear a word against Sir Nigel Gresley, I assert that few men have done greater disservice to British Railways than when he proved to the board of the LNER that they should continue with their policy of steam traction . . . Gresley condemned us to around 2,000bhp when we needed 3,000, for twenty unnecessary years.'[4] The future was elsewhere, notably in the United States, where the new streamlined diesel-electric trains had completely transformed rail travel. By 1934 the *Zephyr* was running at an average of nearly 80mph (128kph) on the journey of nearly 1,000 miles (1,609km) between Chicago and Denver. Moreover, the Germans had also introduced a diesel service, the *Flying Hamburger*, which averaged 74mph (119kph) between Hamburg and Berlin.

But the British showed only limited interest in their continental rivals and in the scientific testing pioneered by the French. This was excusable given that steam power was still capable of considerable development. But even after the war, Robert Riddles, the chief engineer of the newly nationalized British Rail, decided to stick with steam traction. His reasons included a reluctance to rely on imported oil instead of native coal, and the lower capital cost of steam (an argument which pleased the short-termers at the Treasury). But the decision led to disaster, and not only in the delay in converting to diesel. In the mid-1950s, when it was finally decided to phase out steam in favour of diesel, the whole programme was so rushed, and involved so many types of engines, mostly inadequate or unreliable, that it proved far more expensive than the orderly transfer from steam to the mix of electric and diesel practised in better organized countries such as France. Moreover, even the Deltics, the new diesel stars, were based on a lightweight engine originally produced by the German Dornier firm in the late 1920s in an attempt to introduce diesel power in aircraft, and then adapted after the war by the British Napier company for use in fast patrol

Right: **The first public trip of the** *Silver Jubilee,* **inaugurated when King George V celebrated twenty-five years on the throne in 1935. It was this train which set off the Great Train Races of the 1930s. The worthies posing in front of the streamlined** *Silver Link* **engine include the Lord Mayors of London and Newcastle-on-Tyne.**

Previous spread left: **An in-group joke – the poster is a parody of one produced for the Southern Railway promoting much less ambitious journeys.**

Previous spread right: **The real McCoy, or, rather the real** *Mallard,* **Sir Nigel Gresley's Pacific locomotive which established a still-unbeaten world speed record for a steam engine.**

boats. Indeed, only with modernization did speeds start to creep back to the levels reached, albeit only by a handful of special trains, before 1939.

The greatest success of the modernization plan was the electrification of the West Coast Main Line. The decision to electrify was based on considerations which would horrify today's ultracautious British railway planners, but which still make perfect sense. The starting point was the assumption that electrification – as opposed to diesel power, with its lower capital cost but higher running costs (and increased pollution) – was automatically justifiable above a certain traffic threshold. The line's supporters even overlooked the costs of disruption during electrification and the capital cost of fund-

ing the work before the revenue started flowing in. As Roger Ford argues: 'With hindsight, we can say that the financial justification for the WCML electrification was questionable. But electrification reflected the spirit of the times.'[5] In other words, like all great railway schemes before and since, it was an affirmation of faith in the future of the country, and in the communities the railway was designed to serve.

The modernization of the WCML was a major technical achievement involving considerable boldness in fitting a modern power system within a nineteenth-century infrastructure. A fundamental decision was the adoption of alternating current at 25kv to power the trains, rather than the various DC voltages used elsewhere in Britain and in most of the rest of the world. The major exception was France, where an engineering genius called Fernand Nouvion had opted for alternating current when rebuilding France's war-battered railways because it enabled virtually unlimited power to be transmitted with less power loss than with lower voltages, and without the need for most of the expensive apparatus of line-side substations required to convert direct current from industrial voltage. The system may have been undeveloped at the time, but it showed enormous potential – indeed, it is now used to power trains travelling at over 300mph (483kph).

Stanley Warder, BR's chief electrical engineer at the time, was even bolder than Nouvion. He had to be, because on British tracks there was less clearance between the trains and under bridges and tunnels than on the French. Nevertheless, and most dramatically in the tunnels leading down into Euston, he proved that clearances of as low as 2ins (5cm) were safe – a decision which saved several million pounds.

The whole scheme cost a mere £161 million ($241.5 million) (the equivalent today of perhaps £1 billion [$1.5 billion]), and demonstrated that total route modernization, including relaying the tracks and renewing the signalling, was not only practicable but a paying proposition. Within five years – and even before electrification was extended to Glasgow – passenger traffic on the line had doubled, the new system attracting hordes of new passengers as well as former car-users and air devotees. By the mid-1960s, trains were running regularly between London and Crewe at an average of 80mph (129kph), providing a service unequalled on any existing main line in the world.

Yet Warder's achievement was overshadowed by an event which marked the start of the railways' comeback as a modern form of passenger transport. The date of 1 October 1964, when the Japanese National Railway opened their new line between Tokyo and Osaka, remains a crucial one in railway history. The new line did not, in fact, carry trains travelling at an inordinate speed – the average was only 100mph (161kph), 20mph (32kph) faster than BR's trains, which were running on tracks laid down in the 1830s and 1840s. The line's official title, the *Tokaido*, means simply 'Route Number 1' but it is now

known under the unofficial name of *Shinkansen*, meaning simply 'new train'. Not only was it a pioneering line, but it was also the first symbol of Japan's industrial renaissance, a restatement of the original perception of railways as the prime symbol of national technical prowess.

In the thirty-plus years since the opening of the Tokaido line, the building of a new railway has become – as it was 150 years ago – a sign that a country is serious in its efforts to

The LMS's answer to the LNER's streamliners: the *Coronation Scot* photographed in July 1937 six days after breaking the world steam speed record.

Above: **Not fast, but highly economical and convenient. One of British Rail's new multiple units, a 321, able to provide a comfortable, reasonably speedy service on relatively minor lines.**

fuel factor in the transport equation, and thus militated in favour of electricity as the ideal motive power. Early attempts to use hovercraft operating on a cushion of air foundered at the same time. The only competitor now as far as railways are concerned is the use of magnetic force to keep the train above the ground, which could permit speeds of up to 400mph (644kph). The Germans are currently building a completely new line between Berlin and Hamburg based on magnetic levitation, but in developing this system they are unlikely to be able to overcome two inherent problems: the need to build new lines into the heart of the cities being served, which would greatly increase the cost, and the fact that they are aiming at a rapidly moving target – the new French TGVs are running as a matter of course at average speeds of 300kph (186mph), and their latest trains are designed to operate at well over 322kph (200mph).

The *Shinkansen* offered a challenge to other dreamers of railway improvements who had not previously dared to utter their thoughts in public (or felt they would not be taken seriously in the decade of the all-conquering motor car). It also set two other crucial precedents: it provided a regular

become advanced and modern. Yet paradoxically, the basics of railway transport remain unchanged. The new trains are still powered by electric motors and are carried on steel wheels running on steel rails. The old combination has proved far more adaptable than anyone dreamed possible a generation ago, and since then many once-exciting alternatives have fallen by the wayside. This acceptance of the inherent perfectability of well-proven techniques follows the trends in other fields, notably the continued use of the internal combustion engine as the motive power for land-based vehicles, and of such an 'old-fashioned' subsonic aircraft as the Jumbo jet as the standard means of intercontinental transport.

The use of gas turbines or jet engines, which seemed a promising development in the 1960s, was abruptly brought to a halt by the oil crisis of 1973, which promoted the cost-of-

Left: **A very special sort of luggage van. It is called a 'driving van trailer' and is equipped with a driving cab so that the train does not have to be reversed between journeys.**

service, and it democratized speed – the fares, unlike those on the fastest services throughout the history of railways, were no greater than on ordinary trains. For the Japanese had also anticipated another trend, pioneered in Europe by British Rail: the concept that fast trains should not be special but simply a part – often an hourly part – of a regular service. The British name Intercity soon became synonymous with the idea the world over.

Within a year of the opening of the new Tokaido line, the French had produced the first draft of a plan for what was immediately named the TGV, the *train à grande vitesse*, which envisaged a maximum speed of 200mph (322kph) and an average speed of 135–50mph (217–41kph). The obvious candidate for a new line was the route between Paris and Lyons, which, like the original Tokaido line in Japan, was outdated and overcrowded. Moreover, the existing line was a dogleg 320 miles (512km) long. The virtually unlimited power available from electric motors meant that steep gradients were no longer a problem, and so a direct route of a mere 266 miles (425km) was perfectly possible.

By the time the new line was opened in the early 1980s, the distance between the two cities could be covered in two hours (as against the three hours and forty-seven minutes achievable by a single special service, the Mistral, in pre-TGV

Opposite right: **Alas, another Great British Innovation which came to nothing: the tilting train. Unfortunately, the Advanced Passenger Train was sabotaged by BR's more hidebound executives and never got enough backing to make it work properly.**

The Eurostar on its way, not from London Waterloo to Paris or Brussels, but travelling over Chelsea railway bridge on the way to the sidings in west London where it will be cleaned.

days). And the only radically new technology employed was in the signalling. Like the Shinkansen, the TGV was too fast for orthodox line-side signals, so communication had to be by radio. The French also reduced the cost of the project by using 12 miles (19km) of existing tracks out of the Gare de Lyon in Paris and a further few miles on the last stretch into Lyons without incurring too much loss of time. Inevitably, the cost of the line trebled between the drawing up of the first plan at the end of the 1960s and the opening, due to inflation and the cost of electrification (until the oil shock of 1973, the TGV was to have been powered by gas turbines).

As usual, the traffic forecasts proved to have been far too conservative. The SNCF was also pleasantly surprised by the number of passengers who braved the 'three-hour barrier', taking the train on journeys which only partly used TGV, and opting for, say, the three hours and twenty minutes it took to travel from Paris to Geneva or the four and a half hours from Paris to Marseilles by rail rather than by plane. The success

of the TGV Sud-Est line naturally led to pressure from every other French provincial city for a TGV of its own.

Since 1980 a dozen countries have followed the French example, notably the Germans, who are now looking to transform Berlin into the rail capital of Europe: it is the natural centre for rail traffic between Russia, Poland and the west, and from Scandinavia, running through the new tunnels and bridges from Sweden and Denmark, to southern Europe. The Italians dreamed early, but ineffectually. The *direttissimo* (express) designed to run down the peninsula all the way from Milan and Turin to Bologna, Florence, Rome and Naples, was first proposed under Mussolini's regime in 1934. But progress has been episodic, and it was only in late 1992, after most of the work on the Rome–Florence line had been completed, that the authorities gave the go-ahead to the whole project.

The Spaniards, meanwhile, built a totally new line between Madrid and Seville in time for the 1992 Exhibition. This line, originally a purely political gesture, has been a roaring success. It was completed in record time, operates efficiently and, contrary to all predictions, is making a profit. The trend has spread to such aspirants to 'truly advanced' status as Korea, Taiwan and Russia, where the government has formed a joint company to build a new line covering the 408 miles (657km) between Moscow and St Petersburg.

The failure of the British to keep up, and their acceptance of a second-best solution, was revealed in the battle between the tilt train – the ill-fated APT (advanced passenger train) – and the diesel-powered and inappropriately named High-Speed Train, which is in fact capable of only 125mph (201kph), a speed well below those being reached through the use of electric power elsewhere in the world. BR never really believed in the APT. It allocated only a handful of engineers to its development and most of the top brass were not sorry when the prototype had to be withdrawn after only a few days' service, not least because it made everyone sick. So the HSTs won the day, and, after the inevitable teething troubles, they have shown themselves capable of providing reliable and relatively high-speed services on a variety of routes (including those crossing Britain diagonally to avoid London) once the East Coast Main Line from London to Edinburgh had dispensed with their services after electrification. Elsewhere, however, the tilting train, which is able to take corners faster than trains using orthodox suspension techniques, has proved a godsend. It is in use throughout Europe, and is likely to be adopted, belatedly, when the West Coast Main Line is modernized

The modernization of the ECML, a scheme first put forward in the 1950s but only executed in the late 1980s, involved electrifying over 400 miles (644km) of route and 1,200 miles (1,931km) of track (the suburban section, from King's Cross to Hitchin, had already been electrified). In the event, the project took nearly seven years to complete, although, unlike most other major railway enterprises, it came in on budget. It has proved a tremendous success. With modern signalling, and union agreement, there was no reason why the new trains and newly refurbished tracks could not have coped with 140mph (225kph), reducing the journey time to Edinburgh by thirty minutes to three and a half hours. But for a variety of reasons, all of which seem to come back to a lack of national willpower, there still seems little prospect of achieving this target in the near future.

The long drawn-out struggle (there is no other word for it) to update the WCML further illustrates Britain's half-hearted attitude. By the end of the 1980s, the line had become run down, its tracks worn out, its signalling out of date and its services increasingly unreliable. A sane country would have recognized this and embarked on a proper modernization programme immediately after the ECML had been refurbished, and indeed, Dr John Prideaux, the hero of the east-coast scheme, did put forward such an idea, which featured trains and tracks capable of 155mph (250kph) and a consequent reduction in the travelling time to Manchester to under two hours. As things are, the current incredibly and unnecessarily complicated planning process has ensured that the line will not be modernized until the first decade of the twenty-first century, and even then there is no guarantee that it will provide services much faster than those achieved in the mid-1960s.

On other lines, too, Britain's defeatism is bearing fruit, in particular in the form of a phenomenon not seen in any civilized country in recent years: an actual reduction in average speeds. For some years after they were introduced, the HSTs were covering the 111 miles between Paddington and Bristol Parkway in only a few minutes over the hour. Yet the 1996 summer timetable gave a best time of one hour twenty minutes – an average of 83mph (133.5kph), less than double the speeds achieved a century and a half ago. The *Flying Scotsman* took only four hours to reach Edinburgh from London immediately after the ECML had been electrified, yet the time for the 400-mile (644km) trip has now crept up to four hours twelve minutes. This average of a mere 95mph (153kph) falls short of the speeds the Japanese were achieving thirty years ago. The evidence adds up to an institutionalized acceptance of a second-rate status; of a gentle but inevitable decline in Britain's international standing which is, sadly, the hallmark of so many aspects of the country today.

CHAPTER SIX

FROM COAL TO CONTAINERS

IT WAS THE TRAFFIC IN COAL that begat the railways, which, in turn, consumed a substantial proportion of the fuel they carried, although increasingly efficient locomotives demanded correspondingly more combustible 'steam coal'. In the early days, the relationship between the two had its rocky moments. In *The Railway Age*, Michael Robbins describes how a certain company carefully sheeted its coal trucks because it was ashamed of such a low class of traffic.[1] But the British railways soon appreciated the value of their cargo: by 1865 they were transporting 1,700 million tons of coal annually. The difference in cost alone – rail transport was a quarter of the cost of alternative means – accounted for nearly 11.5 per cent of Britain's national income.

The coal wagon in service until relatively recently, which had an opening at the bottom to allow the coal to be dumped more easily, was first developed for use by the Stockton and Darlington Railway. In the 1960s, this idea was developed for the aptly named merry-go-round trains which shuttled between collieries and power stations, discharging their coal automatically through a hopper at the bottom of their wagons. Unfortunately for Britain's railways, the small, unbraked wagons suitable for working round the sharp curves in colliery sidings were retained well into the twentieth century, by which time they were unable to match road transport for speed and efficiency. Other wagons, too, remained unmodernized, the absence of brakes (other than hand brakes) preventing speeds above the merest crawl, until astonishingly recently. The net result – a combination of lack of imagination and lack of investment – was graphically illustrated recently when the American firm Wisconsin Central bought the majority of BR's freight interests. Wisconsin's boss, Ed Burckhardt, took one look at the wagon fleet and promptly declared that the majority of it was fit only for scrap.

Before the arrival of the internal combustion engine, of course, the railways, as the only mechanized form of inland transport, were monarchs of all they surveyed. The consequent extraordinary bustle of traffic was brilliantly described by a contributor to *Railway News* in late 1864. He was writing about St Pancras, but the scene he evoked was being repeated day in, day out in every one of the hundreds of goods yards scattered around Britain.[2]

In the grey mists of the morning, in the atmosphere of a hundred conflicting smells, and by the light of faintly burning gas, we see a large portion of the supply of the great London markets rapidly disgorged by these night trains: fish, flesh and food, Aylesbury butter and dairy-fed pork, apples, cabbages, and cucumbers, alarming supplies of cats' meat, cart loads of water cresses, and we know not what else, for the daily consumption of the metropolis. No sooner do these disappear than at ten minutes' interval arrive other trains with Manchester packs and bales, Liverpool cotton,

Unhurried times: even in 1921 most of the freight being unloaded at the Midland Railway's goods yard at Bradford finished its journey by horse and carriage.

American provisions, Worcester gloves, Kidderminster carpets, Birmingham and Staffordshire hardware, crates of pottery from north Staffordshire, and cloth from Huddersfield, Leeds, Bradford, and other Yorkshire towns, which have to be delivered in the city before the hour for the general commencement of business. At a later hour of the morning these are followed by other trains with the heaviest class of traffic: stones, bricks, iron girders, iron pipes, ale (which comes in great quantities, especially from Allsopps', and the world-famous Burton breweries), coal, hay, straw, grain, flour, and salt.

The heavy casks of beer brewed by increasingly big companies and in demand all over the country, were a natural load for the railways. Indeed, it would be no exaggeration to say that railways were the making of the pale ale first brewed in the Midlands town of Burton-on-Trent in the 1830s. Many of the casks were transported by the Midland Railway to London and stored in the cellars under St Pancras, its London terminus. Every brewery had its own branch line attached to the main line system. As a result Burton-on-Trent was perilously criss-crossed with railways and there were thirty-one level crossings interrupting road traffic. Another danger arose from the custom of offering the train

A Victorian survivor: the oldest standard gauge steam locomotive in Great Britain, an 0–4–0 saddle shunter built in 1863 and still hard at work moving coal for the National Coal Board in 1967.

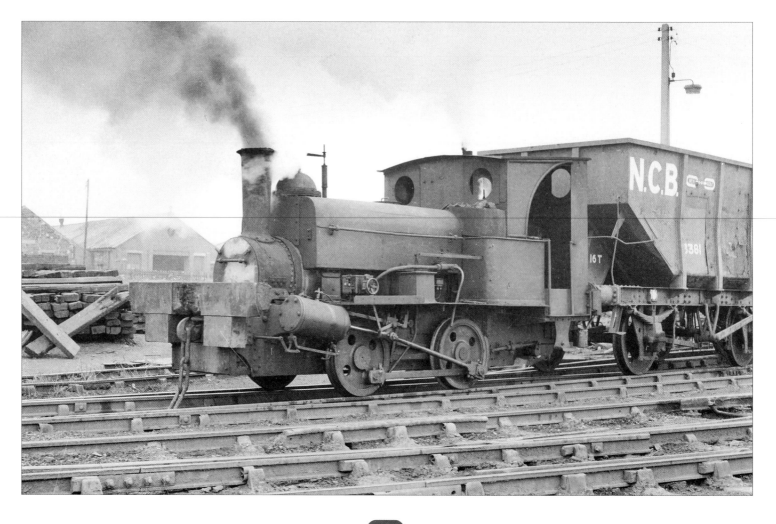

An 0–6–0 colliery locomotive, built by Kitson in 1883, pictured nearly a century later at Derwenthaugh Colliery – typical enough, except that the front wheels were set unusually forward for reasons that remain unclear.

drivers a free glass or two when they arrived at a brewery to collect their loads (and of course, they would visit several breweries in the course of a single shift). The level crossings, like the sozzled drivers, disappeared from the scene when the brewers finally abandoned rail transport in the 1960s.

Two types of freight trains soon developed: the express freight and the incredibly slow 'general'. The special freight trains were reserved for animals – horses, chickens, cows and sheep – and perishable produce like fish, milk, early flowers from Cornwall and the Scilly Isles and fresh fruit and vegetables in season. They also carried newspapers and mail, since the establishment of a nationwide press and a proper national postal system depended on a fast, reliable overnight delivery service. The railways were handling the post by the 1840s, and soon purpose-built carriages were introduced, in which the mail could be sorted overnight, and equipped with dramatic scoops which allowed it to be dumped in special nets by the side of the track at speed. The pioneer of the newspaper special was the eponymous W. H. Smith. In 1847 he chartered a train to deliver the

newspapers from London to Glasgow using the newly opened line beyond Carlisle. Although the last part of the journey had to be made on the turnpike, the point had been made. Two years later, Smith reinforced it with another chartered train which averaged an amazing 49mph (79kph) between London and Edinburgh.

Even before the advent of the railways, London somehow managed to house enough cows to meet the capital's demand for milk, although it was of variable quality. In 1852 *Punch* declared that a clean glass of milk would be one of the seven wonders of London, and asked rhetorically if the metropolis would have to wait until 1922 (the next year when there would be a February with five Saturdays) to enjoy such a luxury. In the event, Londoners only had to wait thirteen years. In 1865, a major outbreak of cattle plague led to a court order for all the cattle in London to be destroyed. There were none of the squabbles which are now a feature of the battle over BSE. 'Within a week,' wrote Bryan Morgan, 'there was not a cow left legally alive within the boundaries of London and the inner home counties. And the capital faced

This Ackerman print, c. 1830, shows that when the Liverpool to Manchester Railway started to run, trains really did carry 'mixed traffic'.

a milk famine.'³ An enterprising dairyman, George Barham, seized the opportunity to bring in supplies of milk by rail from outside London, emphasizing its freshness by naming his company Express Dairies. Barham's initiatives greatly expanded the radius from which London drew its supplies – the Great Western's lines from Berkshire and Wiltshire became known as the Milky Way – and the firm he founded still provides the capital with much of its milk today.

Next to milk, fish was the foodstuff most reliant on the railways. By 1848, Londoners were eating over 70 tons of fresh fish a week brought by rail from Yarmouth and Lowestoft, thus reducing their previous dependence on the smoked or dried variety. Cornish fishermen raced to get their catch to Penzance for the special trains which rushed the fish to Billingsgate, and Aberdeen flourished thanks to the overnight service available to the London market.

In general, however, freight services always suffered because the ablest railwaymen were attracted by the glamour of passenger trains rather than the more mundane, but commercially essential, freight operations. And only a relatively small percentage of freight travelled in fast specials, or, as in the case of express parcels, in the goods vans of passenger trains, a familiar sight until very recently. The majority of freight, like the majority of passengers, trundled along in slower, less glamorous vehicles carrying the 'sundries' – small consignments which were usually trans-shipped more than once in the course of a leisurely journey. What Michael Bonavia says of the Southern was typical of all the networks between the wars. 'A daily pick-up goods train would pursue its leisurely way from station to station shunting for maybe an hour or more at each.'[4] The trip often included what Bonavia calls 'the epitome of the country railway', when a train might

Right: **Boxes of 'choice seedlings' on an early battery-electric truck at Curzon Street Goods Depot in Birmingham in 1928.**

Opposite: **The offices in front of the great Somers Town Goods Yard behind St Pancras station between the wars, when J. Lyons really did live up to their boast of being 'universal caterers'.**

Below: **Roll Out the Barrel: casks of beer on their way to the cellars under St Pancras from the Worthington Brewery at Burton-on-Trent.**

stop in some bosky countryside so that 'a pheasant "shot" with a well-aimed lump of coal could be collected and stored in the footplate tool box'.

These trains would be made up and sent on their way from marshalling yards which were introduced only slowly in Britain. Companies were equally slow to introduce 'gravity' yards with 'humps' in which the wagons could trundle on to their new trains by means of gravity rather than by the use of locomotive power. Even when the British built a theoretically efficient yard, the operations themselves left a lot to be desired. Toton near Nottingham used to be one of the busiest marshalling yards in the world, with a throughput of up to 8,000 wagons every day. Yet veteran drivers remember being stuck in sidings for hours on end. Sometimes a queue of seven or eight trains would be waiting to get into Toton. The result was that 'the railway ran on overtime'. Peter Semmens of the National Railway Museum paints an even bleaker picture: 'Individual wagons could be stuck in vast

marshalling yards for days at a time and it was not uncommon for them to be lost in the system.' When BR launched its modernization programme in 1955, 'Concern was expressed that Great Britain was the only country in the modern world where the majority of freight traffic remained loose-coupled and wagon turnaround times were very poor, averaging 11.9 working days between revenue-earning trips.'[5]

One of the few weapons the railways deployed to any effect in the interwar years in their efforts to fight the implacable advance of the motor lorry was the use of small vans to deliver loads and what we would now call containers to their final destinations. But the railways faced insuperable obstacles in their struggle against the lorry: chronic underinvestment, a totally uncommercial style of management, and, when Dr Beeching came along, a very damaging misunderstanding of the sources of goods traffic. Beeching's closure of dozens of apparently uneconomic depots led to the permanent loss of a great chunk of the railways' freight which had in fact used them. It has not helped that successive governments (most of them, obviously, Conservative) have been in thrall to the preference for roads of the freight-transport lobby. As a result ever larger, grossly undertaxed lorries have infested the roads, while only minimal and grudging help

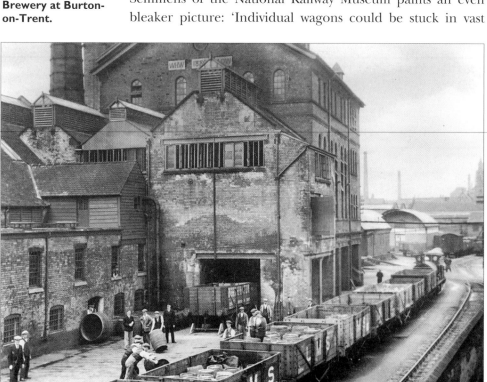

A 112-ton steel ingot being carried from Sheffield to Vickers Armstrong's works in Manchester in 1928 on a special double wagon called a 'gun set'.

has been given to the firms, and the railways, anxious to establish new private sidings for their customers.

The long and mainly unsuccessful war against the motor lorry has left railway companies throughout the world with the need to make a number of basic decisions. The first is the minimum distance over which they can reckon to be truly competitive. In the United States, this generally varies between 500 and 800 miles (805–1,287km), and even in Britain it will never be lower than 200 miles (322km), which in England is further than most industrial hauls, making rail haulage suitable only for runs to and from Scotland and the far north of England. This compares with an average haul for BR's wagons of a mere 67 miles (108km) in 1963 – a year in which the average journey time for freight was two days. There are, of course, a handful of exceptions. The merry-go-round trains running between collieries and power stations will be viable over much shorter distances, as will trains carrying bulk loads of bricks and other building materials.

These 'bulk' trains are one of three types of traffic for which railwaymen are now looking. There are still hopes, notably in Germany, that single wagonloads can be carried competitively, even though the development of 'just-in-time' production techniques has placed an ever-increasing emphasis on speed and reliability, the bugbear of railway freight down the ages. Nevertheless the Germans are investing heavily in marshalling yards – and, more radically, in driverless operation of freight trains.

The big hope for the railway lies in containerization. The modern revolution in freight transport is generally linked with the development of these standardized, easily loadable and unloadable boxes. Such boxes are nothing new: precursors existed on canals in Lancashire before the railway era and were used for many years by the Liverpool and Manchester to carry coal. Between the wars they were further developed in the form of 'conflat' wagons, and after nationalization as Roadrailers and the Freightliner system. But these models required special loading facilities, and recently the hunt has been on for more flexible systems. Today containers come in all shapes and sizes, most familiarly in the form of a trailer carried on a flat car (the 'piggyback system'), and the very similar 'swap bodies', as well as the Roadrailers, trailers which can run on either rail or road.

In principle, the opening of the Channel Tunnel represented a quantum leap in the amount of freight Britain's railways could carry at a competitive price, if only because the average international haul is comfortably above the economic minimum. But the revolution is happening more slowly than anticipated, partly because the price war between the Shuttle and the ferries triggered by the opening of the tunnel has greatly reduced the cost of sending a lorry across the Channel. Nevertheless, a number of multinational companies, notably Ford, have seized the opportunity to use rail for regular shipments of cars – and for transporting parts between their widely scattered factories, such as those in Valencia in southern Spain and Bridgend in south Wales. Originally, BR wanted to channel all the freight traffic

Even in the earliest days of motoring, cars were transported in special vehicles – only in those days the wagons were covered to protect the cars' paintwork.

An 'out of gauge' load (an enormous steel beam), the railways' equivalent of the 'abnormal loads' seen all too frequently on the roads today.

The end of the line for freight in overgrown, neglected marshalling yards.

through a single marshalling yard at Willesden in north-west London, which would have led to unacceptable delays. But even now that the principle of dispersing the freight into a number of yards nearer its final destination has been put into practice, traffic has been slow to build up. This is due to a number of problems, among them the delays imposed by pri-

vatization, the refusal of the British government to convert customers to the idea, and the inability of continental railway companies to take advantage of the opportunities – or, in the case of the French, to allow trains owned by other people to run over their sacred tracks. As a result, the Chunnel has taken longer than expected to reach even its first, modest target of handling 6 million tons of rail freight – three times the weight carried in the special rail ferries used before the tunnel opened.

Because of typical British shortsightedness, two other major opportunities have so far been ignored. The first is the possibility of a corridor of routes, initially from the Channel Tunnel to Glasgow with a branch to Holyhead for traffic destined for Ireland, which could carry full-sized trailers and containers, an idea put forward by the picturesquely named Piggyback Consortium. The improvements required would cost a mere £100 million ($150 million), much of which could come from European funds because of the improvement of the link with Ireland.

While the Piggyback Consortium might eventually get its investment, another, more revolutionary notion has not been properly pursued. It would be faster and more economic for deep-sea cargo ships destined for continental Europe to avoid the Channel on their way to frequently used destinations such as Rotterdam. At least two days could be saved, especially with trans-Atlantic traffic, if the ships were to dock somewhere on the west coast of Britain, the obvious sites being the deep-water facilities at Milford Haven in west Wales and at Hunterston on the west coast of southern Scotland. But, alas, as ever it seems that the imaginations of British businessmen, politicians and civil servants can't be expected to stretch that far.

Left: **One of the faces of modern freight: a train-load of building 'aggregates', like gravel, being unloaded.**

Following spread: **When the Temple Mills marshalling yard near Stratford in east London was built in 1959 with special lighting and 52 miles of track, it was hailed as the solution to BR's freight problems. But yards like this were too slow and unreliable for the demands of modern hauliers.**

CHAPTER SEVEN

MOVING THE MASSES

I N THE BEGINNING was the Metropolitan, the first truly urban railway and the prototype of the world's still-burgeoning band of subways, metros and undergrounds. Before it opened in January 1863, no railway line in the world had ever ventured *through* the heart of a major city. The Metropolitan not only did so, it did so underground. Previously there had been schemes galore, including a madcap proposal by Sir Joseph Paxton, architect of the Crystal Palace, for a Great Victorian Way, an immense avenue of glass 11½ miles (18.5km) long, encircling London with eight railway tracks, four of them for express trains, above an arcade of houses and shops, themselves separated by ordinary railway tracks. The cost was, unsurprisingly, prohibitive, and by the 1850s it was clear that any attempt to build railways of any sort into the heart of London was bound to involve colossal financial investment. It had already cost the poor Great Eastern over £1 million ($1.5 million), an immense sum at the time, to build the last mile of track from Shoreditch into Liverpool Street at the eastern edge of the City of London.

It was no wonder, then, that it took over a decade to raise the money to build the first stretch of the Metropolitan Railway – a mere 3½-mile (5.6-km) track to Moorgate in the city from Bishop's Bridge just west of Paddington Station – designed by Brunel with a view to connecting his trains with those running underground. The project was delayed by the financial strains of the Crimean War and by doubts about the ventilation within the tunnel, despite lofty, and, as it turned out, entirely unjustified, assurances by the engineer, John (later Sir John) Fowler, that the locomotive would either be entirely smokeless or that it would not cause major ventilation problems.

The key to the eventual construction of the Metropolitan Railway was the support of Sir Charles Pearson. He had been a solicitor of the City of London since 1839 and had used his position not only to sort out the City's previously disastrous financial situation but also to campaign incessantly for an improvement in the lot of London's teeming poor. And transport (though not necessarily by railway, above or below ground) played a vital role in his vision. 'A poor man is chained to the spot,' he said in 1846. 'He has not the leisure to walk and he has not the money to ride to a distance from his work.'[1] Later Pearson broadened his view: 'The desire to get out of town is not a mere desire, it is not a passion, it is a disease . . . The passion for country residence is increasing to an extent that it would be impossible for persons who do not mix with the poor to know. You cannot find a place where they do not get a broken teapot in which to stuff, as soon as spring comes, some flower or something to give them an idea of green fields and the country.'

Pearson's ideas chimed with those of other reformers who wanted to introduce 'workmen's fares' to enable the poor to travel on trains – or at least those running early in the morning. But despite the spread of railways, the full implementation

Baker Street station, built in 1863 on the first Underground line in the world, between Paddington and Moorgate. Once the – steam-powered – trains had started to run, the station soon acquired a fine coating of soot which has now been removed, leaving it in pristine condition.

The Victoria Embankment from the City to Parliament Square was built at much the same time as the Metropolitan District Line which ran below it.

of such schemes had to await the development of London's network of municipally owned tramways at the turn of the century, which is described in the next chapter.

The Met may have been an underground railway, but, in an attempt to keep down the construction costs (and in the absence of a satisfactory tunnelling machine), it was built by the cut-and-cover method. Holes were dug, the sides shored up and brick walls and arches constructed. In fact there was only one tunnel on the route, and that was a mere 742yds (678m) long. To minimize the cost and the disturbance, the whole line was built under the streets, as was the Paris Metro nearly half a century later.

The Met was, of course, powered by steam, and despite the blowholes and special (allegedly unsmoky) locomotives, both passengers, and to an even greater extent, staff were bound to suffer from respiratory diseases. When Max

Beerbohm was a theatre critic and had to review some appalling play, he used to say to himself, 'At least I am not a porter on the Metropolitan Railway.'

The years after the Met was opened were inauspicious, to say the least, for railway-builders. Between 1864 and 1866, the attempts of a number of companies to gain access to the City (or, in one case, through the heart of the City via the Snow Hill tunnel between Blackfriars and Farringdon) led to the Overend Gurney crisis, the worst of many in the financial fortunes of the nineteenth century. But the Met spread its wings, as did the District Line – initially its partner and subsequently its rival – in their efforts to build a line encircling central London, linked to other routes, some on the surface, some just below. In the 1870s and 1880s the Metropolitan Line was galvanized by the dreams – call them megalomaniacal, or, more positively, a century ahead of their time – of its chairman, Sir Edward Watkin. His plans involved combining the Met with his other companies, which ran what became the Great Central, extending from Marylebone Station near Baker Street northwards to Sheffield. This line was constructed to allow the broader and taller trains used on the continent to run on British rails, for Watkin's ultimate ambition was to link the Great Central with a Channel tunnel.

The Met's ambitions were more modest, but it did succeed in coping with the way that Londoners, more than the inhabitants of any other city in the world, became almost fanatical commuters, willing to spend four or five hours a day travelling to and from work in an increasingly frantic effort to escape beyond the city to create their own rural idyll. This escapism into a largely imaginary past was reflected by the spread of the Met, first into suburbia, and then far out into the countryside into what can only be termed exurbia. The Met was able to take full and profitable advantage of this flight from the city because it was the only British railway company which had the right to develop settlements on its own land. In the first forty years of this century it capitalized on its position, and as a result the word Metroland came into being to describe a number of leafy suburbs.

From Baker Street the Met expanded out into the peaceful Buckinghamshire countryside, reaching Chesham in 1889 and Aylesbury, over 35 miles (56km) from London, three years later. At its zenith – and indeed, until a few years before the Second World War – it ran services as far as Verney Junction on the Oxford to Bletchley line. Between the First World War and 1939 it offered a Pullman-car service, for which a supplement to the first-class fare had to be paid, and which was popular with wealthy commuters and theatregoers. And there was even a private car (belonging to Lord Rothschild, whose country house at Wendover was served by the line) which could be called into service when the Pullman was out of action.

By 1875 the District Railway, an early element in London's Underground network, had tunnelled to within a few hundred yards of St Paul's Cathedral.

In technical terms, the Met was conservative: while the rest of the underground system had been electrified by 1905, the Met stuck to steam for its suburban services beyond Harrow-on-the-Hill and Rickmansworth. Indeed, electrification did not finally arrive at Amersham and Chesham until 1961. Up to 1962 the Met also owned some splendid electric locomotives with such names as *Sherlock Holmes* (Baker Street station is only a few yards from 221b Baker Street, the fictional home of the famous detective). The single survivor, the *Sarah Siddons*, is still a favourite among lovers of vintage locomotives.

It took two major technical advances to enable Londoners to travel by rail through the heart of the city, for the cut-and-cover construction method was clearly impractical for the centre itself. The first was the development of the electric motor. By 1890, Dr Siemens had demonstrated his system in Berlin and Magnus Volk had built a little electric railway on Brighton seafront. At the same time, a new tunnelling method had made it possible for tunnels to be built deep underground. The concept of digging behind an iron shield had originally been tested by Marc Brunel, Isambard's father, in his heroic efforts to construct the first Thames tunnel during the 1820s and 1830s. But the experiment had been so drawn-out and so costly in terms of both money and lives that it was never going to be repeated in the same form. The first step forward came in the 1860s, when a little-known engineer, Peter William Barlow, conceived the idea of laying the hollow cylindrical piers he was using on a new bridge not vertically but horizontally. He developed a new type of shield which had a cast-iron cutting edge, 7ft (2.13m) across, with a face plate – a sort of waterproof sliding door – behind it. The shield was moved methodically forward by screw jacks, which enabled the miners to cut away the dirt by hand, leaving the new excavation to be lined with iron plates bolted together. In 1870 Barlow first tried out his innovation when building a small tunnel under the Thames near the Tower of London. Technically it was a success, although the tunnel itself was a commercial failure since it could not compete once Tower Bridge was constructed.

By 1906 what was to be known as the Piccadilly Line was already electrified. By 1939 it extended out to Cockfosters in the east and to Hounslow in the west – and by 1977 the line was serving Heathrow Airport.

Barlow's ideas were taken a stage further by James Henry Greathead, who, in 1884, began to build the first 'tube' from King William Street near the Bank of England under the Thames to the Elephant and Castle, using hydraulic jacks and a mechanical digger which tore out the clay and evacuated it into an endless chain of buckets. Compressed-air airlocks kept the water at bay. The new 'tube', the City and South London, was opened by the Prince of Wales, later King Edward VII, in 1890.

Over the years, the line was altered and extended until it finally became the Northern Line, which boasts the longest urban underground tunnel in the world – it stretches for 27 miles (43km) from Golders Green in the north to Morden in the south. A more important development was the opening in 1900 of the first section of the Central Line, initially from Shepherds Bush to the Bank. This was the famous 'tuppenny tube' – the first example of a flat-fare policy. The Central-Line trains were more inviting than the underpowered ones on the City and South London, whose carriages were known as 'padded cells'. Originally, they had no windows and even the later trains had only small, frosted ones right at the top. The trains on the Central Line had proper windows, and the stations were clean, white-tiled and brightly lit.

The Great Northern, Piccadilly & Brompton Railway.

WARNING!

ELECTRIC TRAINS
WILL COMMENCE RUNNING DAILY ON
MONDAY, DECEMBER 3rd, 1906,
Every few minutes the entire length of the
EAST and WEST BOUND ROADS from
5.0 a.m. to 1.0 a.m.

Men are warned to keep clear of the TRACKS & TUNNELS during these hours.

BY ORDER.

PICCADILLY CIRCUS OFFICE,
November 24th, 1906.

TUBE STATION SHEPHERDS BUSH.

Shepherds Bush station on the original 'Tuppenny Tube' now known as the Central Line. For 2d, less than one new penny, you could travel right across London.

The Central Line and the other lines proposed or built around the turn of the century would never have been combined into an integrated network had it not been for the manoeuvrings of an American wheeler-dealer called Charles Tyson Yerkes, the model for the evil financier in Theodore Dreiser's famous and influential trilogy of 'muck-raking' novels. After being chased out of Chicago, having overstepped the mark in his attempts to defraud its inhabitants, he fled to Europe and began a campaign to establish the sort of monopoly over London's urban transport that he had built up in Chicago, and before that, in Philadelphia. As it turned out, Londoners were lucky. Yerkes died in 1905, having brought together most of the lines in a dodgy holding company financed mostly by American money. As a result, London found itself with a sensible system (its only major disadvantage was the small size of the tunnels) acquired at virtually no cost to the taxpayers (or British investors, for that matter).

The development of the tube, of motor buses, and of electric trams made the last four years of the nineteenth century and the years leading up to the First World War the period during which Londoners really became mobile. The annual number of journeys made by the average Londoner nearly doubled, to 300, in those seventeen years, and the number of rail trips jumped from 400 million to 710 million.

In the next half-century several lines, notably the Central in Essex and the Northern and Bakerloo in north-west London, followed in the footsteps of the Met, and of London's tramway system, in extending the city's boundaries by providing cheap and reliable transport to settlements such as Hendon and Stanmore, which remained surprisingly rural until the 1930s. Unlike in Paris, where the whole system was developed in one astonishing burst around the turn of the century and then remained virtually untouched until the 1970s, progress in London was more

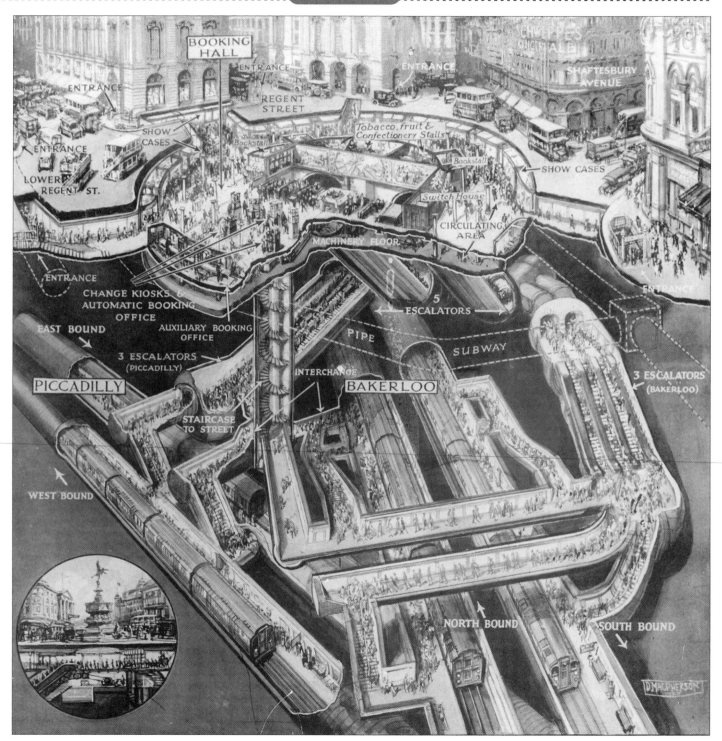

BOOKING HALL

ENTRANCE

ENTRANCE

SHAFTESBURY AVENUE

ENTRANCE

REGENT STREET

ENTRANCE

SHOW CASES

Tobacco, fruit & Confectionery Stalls

Bookstall

Bookstall

SHOW CASES

LOWER REGENT ST.

Switch House

CIRCULATING AREA

MACHINERY FLOOR

ENTRANCE

ENTRANCE

CHANGE KIOSKS & AUTOMATIC BOOKING OFFICE

AUXILIARY BOOKING OFFICE

5 ESCALATORS

EAST BOUND

PIPE

SUBWAY

3 ESCALATORS (PICCADILLY)

INTERCHANGE

BAKERLOO

3 ESCALATORS (BAKERLOO)

PICCADILLY

STAIRCASE TO STREET

WEST BOUND

NORTH BOUND

SOUTH BOUND

D. MACPHERSON

A modern marvel in 1928, Piccadilly station, the model for such interchanges the world over.

Following page: **An early version of the map of London's Underground system shows its spread more clearly than the later, more famous, and more schematic version.**

Left: **Controlling the current. By 1932 it took only one – relaxed – chap in plus-fours to look after the electricity supply for the whole of the eastern half of the Piccadilly Line.**

episodic. There was a flurry of activity in the 1930s, although some of the extensions planned then were not completed until after the last war. Then there was a fallow period until the Victoria Line was built in the late 1960s, relieving the strain on the Piccadilly Line and extending the tube to a number of impoverished north-eastern suburbs. Over a decade later came the Jubilee Line, which took in the Stanmore branch of the Bakerloo Line. The Jubilee Line is now being extended from the West End, along a route designed to serve the developments at Canary Wharf in a classic case of political expediency (former prime minister Margaret Thatcher's desire to accommodate the developers) taking precedence over considerations of transport planning. In its favour it has to be said that the line will open up a previously rather isolated part of south-east London.

The 1930s were the great days of London's tube system, the days of Lord Ashfield and Frank Pick, when the network set a

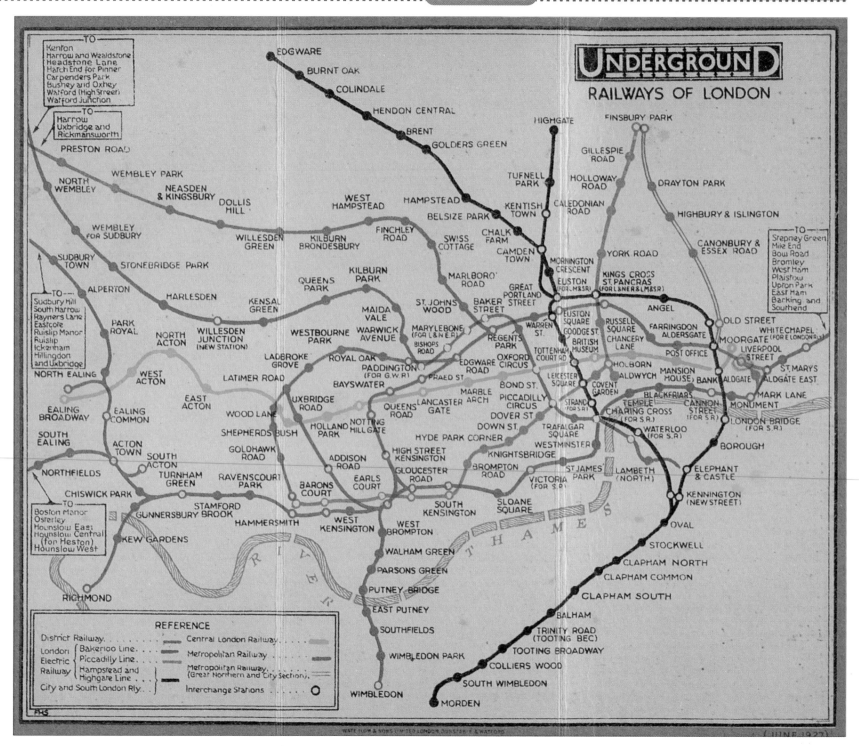

standard unequalled at the time by any urban transport system anywhere in the world. Ashfield, born Albert Stanley in the United States, was an outstanding businessman and diplomat who drew together the whole of London's passenger transport system – tubes, buses and trams (and later trolleybuses) – under the aegis of the London Passenger Transport Board, a model of municipal ownership. This innovation owed much to Charles Yerkes' attempt to create a cartel, but even more to the feeling prevalent in the late 1920s that joint ownership and development of such important national assets as the national electricity grid was better than pure capitalism.

Frank Pick, the managing director of the newly formed London Passenger Transport Board, instituted a unified design policy which remains the envy of the world. The trains, the advertising and the stations on the tube's new extensions, and the many new escalators throughout the system, were all in keeping with an overall style, a package of clean but unintimidating design which invited passengers to use what was obviously the most modern form of transport available – in effect glamorising, making fashionable, the normally humdrum business of travelling around a major city.

Since the 1930s it has not exactly been downhill all the way, but after the war London ceased to be the cynosure it once was, and it has gradually been overtaken by a number of other cities, notably Paris, in terms of new routes and modernization. The nadir was a dreadful period in the 1970s and 1980s when the whole system was allowed to run down. It is only in the 1990s that the situation has improved, but the long-overdue modernization of the network and refurbishment of many shabby stations still has a long way to go. This would have involved far less disruption had it been carried out in a more orderly fashion over a longer period.

London's first underground railway, the Metropolitan Line, was not the first to bring passengers into town. The concept of commuting (though not the word itself, which was, like so many other new terms, coined in the States) was introduced by wealthy travellers on the London to Brighton line as soon as it was opened in 1841, and to this day the line remains the archetype of the commuter railway. Its electrification formed

9

SUTTON
VIA SELHURST

the heart of one of the most ambitious investments undertaken between the wars. Indeed, until after 1945, British railway electrification was almost entirely confined to the commuter routes of the Southern Railway, the smallest (in terms of share capital as well as in miles of track) of the big four into which the country's hundreds of railway companies were grouped in 1923.

The Southern was spurred on by a steady increase in the number of commuters, by the success of London's electric tramway system in attracting passengers from the railways in south London and by the ambitious electrification scheme launched in the first decade of the century by the London, Brighton and South Coast Railway, using highly advanced German AC technology at 6,600 volts, which had been scuppered by the First World War.

Unlike the other three groups, the Southern depended very largely on revenue from passengers, which constituted up to three quarters of its total, as opposed to freight. Not only did it carry the bulk of London's commuters, but it also ferried millions of holidaymakers to resorts on the south coast, troops to and from innumerable barracks and racegoers and 'sportsmen' to the twenty-three racecourses it served, including Epsom and Ascot. In addition to the pressure of growing passenger traffic, the SR's electrification programme – the most ambitious in the world at the time – was due in no small part to the efforts of Sir Herbert Walker, who presided over the company for fifteen of its twenty-five years of existence (it was swallowed up by BR in 1948). He transformed the three warring companies which made up the Southern into a (more or less) unified whole and created that rarest of phenomena in the railway world, an orderly management structure. The fact that he had inherited a chaotic muddle of mostly outdated locomotives and rolling stock was a further catalyst for the idea of electrification.

Electrification received a considerable boost with the abolition of railway passenger duty in 1929, on condition that the money saved would be spent on capital works. The Southern Railway duly spent the £2 million ($3 million) it

Previous spread, right: **As early as 1910 this poster, entitled 'Too Much of a Good Thing' showed that London Underground was competing vigorously with the capital's tramway system in enticing London's millions into what became the Green Belt.**

Left: **The tiny Surrey station of Carshalton Beeches was served by an early example of Southern Railway electrification, the Norwood Junction West Croydon and Sutton line.**

That'll be the day.

received, as well as its own reserves and finance generated by low-cost loans from the government-sponsored Railway Finance Corporation, on electrifying much of its network. But in one important respect Walker and his advisers remained conservative: they stuck to trains powered by DC motors, which drew their current from a third rail, preferring to expand the sketchy network of lines near London electrified at 600 volts DC during the First World War, rather than considering the still relatively untried AC system pioneered by the LB&SC before 1914. This approach, with the emphasis on the pragmatic and the economic rather than the technically daring, was typical of the whole attitude of the SR, though there were exceptions. The colour signalling installed on the newly electrified routes was far in advance of its time, and in another respect, too, Walker was a firm innovator. Michael Bonavia records that he 'believed firmly in frequent services, especially off-peak even where poor loadings might have tempted a reduction in frequency'.[2] Walker provided a 'clockface' facility, with trains on the hour, half-hour and quarter-hour. This regularity was designed to attract what were then called 'season-ticket holders', the term used before the American word 'commuter' gained currency in England.

Although there was some extension of the electrified routes in the 1920s, the key to the scheme was the London to Brighton line. In the early 1930s, this was transformed by a thorough modernization programme which included improvements to stations, track and signalling. The Brighton line was crucial – not only because it was the best known, and, with the Pullman *Brighton Belle*, the most glamorous of all the commuter lines, but also because it set a pattern of modernization without frills, and without truly up-to-date rolling stock. For the scheme made use of stock which dated back to the 1920s – only a few lucky passengers had access to toilets, for instance – even though these carriages were destined to trundle up and down the line for the next thirty-five years.

The Pullman, however, was something special. For nearly ninety years, the London–Brighton line had been one of the few in the world on which well-off commuters could find the sort of comfort to which they were accustomed on their longer railway journeys. (The only others were on a handful of routes out of New York.) The Southern didn't let down their customers. They built three trains of all-steel construction with fine marquetry work inside the carriages, designed to propel the *City Limited*, as it was then known, at up to 75mph (121kph), a speed that was certainly often exceeded.

The new Pullman, called the *Southern Belle* before assuming its better-known name, *Brighton Belle*, in June 1934, was the first all-Pullman electric multiple unit and retained a magic all its own for the next forty years – so much so that it out-lived its viability by a long chalk. Its users clung to the fast-disappearing luxury of a bygone age – in the autumn of the *Belle*'s career, the proposal to withdraw kippers from the

Left: **The only truly glamorous commuter train in the world changed its name from the *Southern Belle* to the *Brighton Belle* in 1934 and was not withdrawn until 1972 when the original rolling stock wore out. In 1997 the name was revived to promote a new fast service doing the 54-mile journey in 47 minutes.**

Opposite: **By 1984 Londoners were becoming used to what was originally called the Denver Clamp, and London Underground was quick to seize on the advantages this gave public transport – although the Thatcher government ensured that it was much slower to provide new trains.**

Opposite: **The first urban railway in the world, the London to Greenwich line, built in 1836 and not much improved since.**

Below: **Fenchurch Street station, the only main-line station in London not served by the Underground, and the terminus of the infamous London Tilbury and Southend line.**

breakfast menu caused a storm of protest – but with its thirty-five attendants, fourteen of whom were on duty at any one time, the *Belle* had been thoroughly uneconomic for many years before it was finally withdrawn on 30 September 1972. Even today there is a flagship train of the same name, whose journey time is due to be reduced to under fifty minutes in the next couple of years.

During the 1930s, the lines to Portsmouth, Littlehampton, Tunbridge Wells and Chatham, as well as much of the line along the south coast, all received the electrification treatment. The ensuing dramatic increase in traffic was partly due to the increased comfort, accelerated journeys and more frequent trains (four expresses an hour to Portsmouth in holiday periods) modernization brought, but also to the enormous boom in house-building in southern England during what was, for the southern middle classes anyway, a decade of relative prosperity. Yet the accommodation remained pretty poor. The trains built for the newly electrified lines to Maidstone and Rochester were called HALs. As Michael Baker reveals, 'This, believe it or not, meant "half a lavatory"' – in other words, 'only half the passengers in each unit had access to the lavatory . . . The HALs were designed by Oliver Bulleid, the Southern's notoriously egotistical chief engineer, and were a foretaste of his notion of packing in as many passengers as possible regardless of comfort, which reached its full and ghastly fruition in his first suburban units two years later.'[3]

Sir Herbert Walker was hampered by a rather cowardly board, and as a result his programme was executed on what now seems like the proverbial shoestring. Two years after his retirement in 1937, the war prevented any further progress. Under nationalization, electrification was a lot more patchy, undertaken in fits and starts. It was not begun again at all until BR's modernization programme was launched in the late 1950s. This took electric trains to Folkestone and Dover in the east (a rare case of a total modernization scheme for a whole network), and, in the late 1960s, to Bournemouth.

Nationalization notwithstanding, the Southern (now a mere region rather than a railway) retained what Baker calls its 'predilection for taking two steps forward and one step back . . . some of its trains were built on underframes from withdrawn 2NOLs – in other words, a fair part of them dates back to the 1930s. The Southern Electric is a most frugal concern which has always got its money's worth out of everything it owns.' Baker further remarks that the units used on the Bournemouth line, itself a 'pretty cut-price second-rate affair . . . achieved the interesting (though not in Southern terms unique) feat of being both revolutionary and antiquated at the same time'. As was only to be expected, then, the older stock was refurbished rather than replaced during the 1970s and 1980s, and even though the prototypes of trains with sliding

The drama of electrification: the Kent Coast line at Shortlands in south-east London at the end of May 1959.

doors – a vast and crucial improvement leading to less noise and less time wasted at stations – appeared in 1971, it will be well into the twenty-first century before all the older 'slam-door' stock is replaced. There is a striking contrast here with the way that, before the war, the LNER planned (and BR executed after 1945) the electrification of its routes from Liverpool Street into Essex. Their rolling stock featured power-operated doors and open carriages rather than the compartments into which the Southern traditionally crammed its passengers.

A third burst of electrification had in the late 1980s filled in most of the gaps, notably the lines to Hastings and Weymouth. It also led to the introduction of the type 442s, better known as Wessex Electric trains, which gave travellers on the Southern line the chance to ride in truly modern trains, perhaps for the first time ever.

Unfortunately, BR's regionalization had led to the abandonment of the notion that trains could run right through London. The Snow Hill Tunnel, the crucial link between north and south, had been much used by trains running on such unlikely routes as Enfield to Woolwich, as well as for the highly popular service of fifty trains a day between Moorgate and Victoria. But passenger traffic stopped in the First World War, and the tunnel was abandoned altogether in 1969 because it joined two regions uninterested in cross-London travel.

In the late 1980s, however, it was revived, with the help of new rolling stock capable of coping with the two different power supplies involved (750DC to the south; 25,000 volts AC to the north). The tunnel immediately became the lynchpin of a series of services linking the Brighton line – including, and most importantly, Gatwick Airport – with north London and the suburban lines to Luton and Bedford. With the completion of a number of much-delayed improvements lumped together under the name Thameslink 2000, these connections will be far more solid, and will make it possible, in theory at least, to run trains from all over southern England to any destination that will attract traffic. However, it will be even more difficult to set up such links, now that the catchment area is served by half a dozen separate and often competing companies, than it was when the Thames alone marked the boundary between a mere two of BR's regions.

The histories of other commuter lines round London, such as the Midland to Luton and Bedford, the Great Northern to Cambridge and the Great Eastern to Chelmsford and Colchester, tend to mirror that of British railways in general rather than the specific experience of the Southern. Of course, they've all been starved of investment, but when they have been modernized it has been in a more thoroughgoing fashion than has been the case with the lines south of the Thames (although the Great Eastern did make a false start by electrifying initially at 1500 volts). And the modernization of one of them did not involve electrification at all. The Chiltern line – in effect, the outer half of the old Metropolitan system – was hopelessly neglected between 1960 and 1990. Indeed, the engines were so old that spare parts became virtually unobtainable. But in a single burst, the whole network has recently been brought up to date, with the result that, not only has traffic on the basic system from Marylebone, Sir Edward Watkin's memorial, to High Wycombe, Aylesbury and Banbury greatly increased, but the new operators are also planning to compete with new diesel units capable of 100mph (161kph) on the route to the hitherto neglected towns between Banbury and Birmingham.

But there is one line that stands apart, both literally and metaphorically. For nearly 150 years, the London, Tilbury and Southend Railway has been the unwanted orphan among commuter lines, and has many times justified its claim to the title 'Misery Line'. And yet it has had a greater social effect than any other single piece of track round the metropolis.

The line to Tilbury opened in 1854 and reached Southend two years later. From the start it was a separate line, 45 miles (72.5km) long, and it is perhaps symbolic that it started from Fenchurch Street, the only London terminus not served by the underground. It was built – by the famous contractors Brassey, Peto and Betts – in conjunction with their development of Clifftown, a new part of Southend, complete with its own lift to the beach, which is now a conservation area.

The line came of age with two developments. First the introduction of bank holidays in 1871 led to an influx of day trippers travelling from London's East End to Southend (by 1874, troops had to be brought out to stop them rioting). By the mid-1930s, up to 45,000 Londoners would flood back home every Sunday evening in the summer and up to 70,000 on bank holidays. Of more regular importance were the 12,000 season-ticket holders created by the steady spread of the population eastwards from London – the trend so fervently desired by pioneers like Sir Charles Pearson in order to get the workers out of the slums. In the 1920s this resulted in the building of some massive council estates along the route by the London County Council, including the Becontree estate, the largest in the world, which, by 1934, comprised 35,000 houses. These housing estates were further encouraged by the expansion of the mighty Ford plant at Dagenham in the fifteen years after it was established in 1924.

But the LTS was a solitary, almost detached branch of the Midland, and then the LMS, to which it had only the most tenuous connection, basically through freight traffic to the docks at Tilbury. Consequently, it always suffered from the fact that a much more comprehensive network, the Great Eastern (subsequently the LNER), ran northwards almost parallel to its own competing route to Southend.

The neglect was so bad that after 1945, commuters made a series of well-publicized protests. They formed themselves into the County Borough of Southend-on-Sea Railway Travellers' Association, a well-orchestrated pressure group which even had its own highly professional magazine. They were taken seriously enough: in February 1949 their representatives were received by Sir Eustace Missenden, Walker's successor on the Southern line and at the time chairman of the Railway Executive. The whole affair had its comic aspects. When the association sent Missenden a telegram congratulating him on the fact that one particular commuter train had arrived punctually for the first time in six months, the authorities took issue with them, claiming that it had in fact arrived on time on no fewer than nine separate occasions in under two months. Naturally, the problems bred legends and the sort of grim humour characteristic of Britons faced with apparently insuperable hardships. The trains were so crowded that some ladies sat regularly on chaps' laps, and another part of the train was taken over by card-players occupying themselves during the inevitable delays.

The commuters had plenty to complain about, too. There were not enough trains, and those there were were unpunctual; as well as a shortage of reliable locomotives some were hand-me-downs from richer lines. But help was at hand, albeit not from official sources. A young electrical engineering student, Barry Flaxman, did a thorough study of the line and confirmed a host of inadequacies. An average of nine locomotives were out of action every day; trains were held up to have their windows closed; a spare track was not being used for fast trains. Flaxman came up with a new timetable based on Sir Herbert Walker's 'clockface' principle, which, unbelievably, was accepted.

After all this, the principle of electrification of the LTS, using the same 1,500DC system being incorporated on the Great Eastern, was at last agreed. It had been proposed by the Midland as far back as 1913. But it took another decade of steadily rising traffic, generated by further expansion of existing towns and the establishment of the new town at Basildon (which at first didn't even have a station), before this took place, and even then the signalling installed back in the 1930s was not renewed. It was eventually replaced in the 1990s, while some newish, albeit second-hand, trains are being bought since the line was privatized. The buyers promptly floated the company on the Stock Exchange. The shares promptly rose vertiginously, an echo of the boom that marked the early days of railways 150 years ago.

CHAPTER EIGHT

FROM TRAMS TO LIGHT RAIL

T HAT USEFUL BEAST the tram has always been underestimated, if not scorned, in Britain, whereas in many countries on the continent it has remained an essential element of the urban scene for nigh on a century. Town buses can cope with only 6,000 passengers per direction per hour, and economically it is difficult to justify the construction costs of a special metro system for traffic of a density much below 20,000ppdph. Trams can fill the very considerable gap between the other two systems.

Trams, or light railways, as they are now called, are a special breed. David Holt describes them as 'neither a train in the street, nor a bus on rails . . . a distinct form of transport in its own right, a rail vehicle with some of the characteristics of a road vehicle . . . a free-range railway, a railway unconstrained by fixed ideas . . . domesticated and able to run sociably at will among its patrons in their own environment.'[1]

Enthusiasm for this uniquely friendly means of transport may be limited by the fact that the tram is, technically, not a very interesting machine, but most importantly, perhaps, by its association with the urban proletariat in teeming slums. It was therefore a prime target for the urban 'improvers' of postwar Britain, who were anxious to remove every trace of such associations from our urban past. In doing so they replaced dozens of handsome, 'user-friendly' town centres with shoddy, soulless shopping centres surrounded by brutal, intrusive, ring roads eternally crowded with noisy, polluting vehicles. Today, as we repent of our postwar ways and try to restore the peace and humanity of our towns and cities, we are coming to realize that the tram can once again play an important role. For it remains a superb means of urban transport: immensely efficient, a non-polluter, and, even though it was condemned as intrusive, far less so than its replacements, the motor bus and private car.

In its earlier life the tram was a much more vital thread in the fabric of urban life in Britain for half a century than ordinary railways, which, as we have seen, often did not penetrate into the centres of towns and cities. So inevitably, railways made only a limited impact on the life of the city, and even less of one as a means of freeing the poor from their ghettos. Electric trams were the only real contact the urban working classes had with any form of railway, for commuting has always been essentially a middle-class phenomenon. Fortunately, today Britain is creeping back into the civilized world and bringing back the tram, albeit under a new, sanitized, modern-sounding name: the light railway.

Like the first railways, the first trams, introduced in about 1860, were horse-drawn, and relied on the same principle: that there was less friction between a wheel made of iron or steel and a rail made of the same material than there was between a wheel (in those days wooden or iron) and the rough cobblestones with which virtually all city streets were paved. By 1883 they were carrying 300 million passengers a year, and at their peak some ten years later, when there was 1,000 miles (1,609km) of steam-driven tram track as well,

The trams in all their glory, a herd of giant electric beasts at the Elephant and Castle in south London in 1922.

The steam tram was naturally unpopular and dirty, polluting the streets of London as in other cities where it was tried until superseded by electrically-powered vehicles.

they were handling double that number. But horse-drawn trams had clear limitations: they were slow and the relatively high fares ensured that, like the trains, they were used primarily by the middle classes.

And the new steam-powered trams were not a great success. They frightened the horses, which remained the dominant motive power, and the inhabitants of the more respectable roads they served were put off by how dirty they were. In the words of A. Winstan Bond, 'They were really equivalent to bringing the industrial revolution into the better part of town.'[2] Nevertheless, 'The steam tram did establish the principle of mechanical traction on the road', and represented

something of a comeback after the comprehensive defeat of the London-based road-engine manufacturers by the northerners, led by George Stephenson at Rainhill half a century earlier.

With the development of the electric motor in the late 1870s came new possibilities. The first idea was cable cars, powered through an endless cable on a drum run by electric motors. The driver simply had to hitch his machine to the cable by clamping and unclamping it. These 'street funiculars' were reportedly invented by an anonymous Scotsman horrified at the suffering of horses on hilly tram routes. Indeed, they were used mostly in hilly cities like Edinburgh and Llandudno, and so it is not surprising that the only remaining examples are to be found in a handful of particularly hilly cities like Lisbon and San Francisco. A variety of other means of transmitting the power were tried. Birmingham was one of the few cities to use batteries, even though they were heavy, cumbersome and short-lived. Many others, especially London, avoided the use of awkward overhead wires by transmitting the power either through conduits buried in slots in the rail or occasionally through electrified metal studs placed along the route.

Back in 1891, Leeds was the first major city to introduce a tramway system using electrified overhead wires, and most other British towns and cities soon followed suit. They were well behind the Americans, who had over 12,000 miles (29,312km) of electrically driven tramways by 1896. Britain also lagged behind the Germans, and as a result most of the country's equipment was either imported from the United States or made by British-based subsidiaries of German or American firms like Siemens and Westinghouse.

These subsidiaries flourished as a result of a miraculous burst of construction. While only forty electric tram systems had been established by 1900, 102 were built between 1901 and 1904, and a further thirty-nine in the ten years before the outbreak of the First World War. Municipalities were

A Bank Holiday crowd in 1919, the first after the Great War, in an era when trams were the best and cheapest means of escape from urban grime.

Opposite: **The arrival of the first electric trams in south London in 1903 was (rightly) recognized as a major event in parts of the city previously served only by (relatively costly and infrequent) trains.**

Below: **Fit for a secular shrine: a silver model of one of the first electric trams, which ran in Bristol as early as 1901.**

especially keen on tramways because they were profitable enough to cover the losses incurred by the generators they used for lighting their streets. Moreover, the British benefited from being ten years behind the Americans, for in the meantime the cost of construction had fallen by a third and that of electric motors by two thirds.

Some of these systems were enormous. Manchester's topped the table, partly because its railway network served three different and unconnected stations in the centre of the city. From these the tram system spread throughout what we would now call the south Lancashire conurbation, north to Bolton, south to Stockport, and west to St Helen's, where you could catch a connecting tram to Liverpool, in an echo of

the pioneering Liverpool to Manchester railway. Birmingham's network spread just as widely, throughout the Black Country to Wolverhampton. By 1914 there were 180 systems in 150 towns and cities, large and small. In 1900 passenger numbers already exceeded those travelling third class on the country's railways, and by 1910 trams were carrying three times as many. For the electric tram served as a major liberating force for the urban working classes, enabling them to travel further and cheaper, not only to and from work, but also to escape from their urban ghettos into the countryside.

Technically, the trams were simplicity itself, usually running on a 4ft 8⅜in (1,241mm) gauge, or sometimes on a narrower one of 3ft 6ins (930mm). The driver had to use only two levers: one to put the tram into forward or reverse; the other to regulate, originally through a series of notches, the amount of current being passed to the motors, and thus the vehicle's speed. Nevertheless, driving a tram was not as simple as it might appear: it could get decidedly tricky on slopes, up and down, in wet weather, when sand to maintain grip on the rails had to be available, and at the numerous crossings and points in town centres. It was there, of course, that the danger of accidents was at its greatest, and their relative infrequency speaks volumes for the drivers' skills, and for the natural awe in which these lumbering beasts were held by pedestrians, cyclists and even motorists.

Throughout the rise and decline of the tram, its technical aspects remained largely unchanged. A number of electric motors, together with their running gear, were slung within and below four-wheel bogies, called 'trucks', on which the tram's body was built – a design originally patented by an American engineer, J. G. Brill. However big the tram, the loads on every axle, and thus on the rails and road bed, were far lower than those imposed by lorries carrying (heavy) freight rather than (relatively light) human beings.

Of course, there were developments. Originally, the motors (generally two of 25bph each were employed) were large and heavy, their size increased by the need for large casings to provide room for the heat to dissipate in the absence of forced ventilation. With the advent of better ventilation,

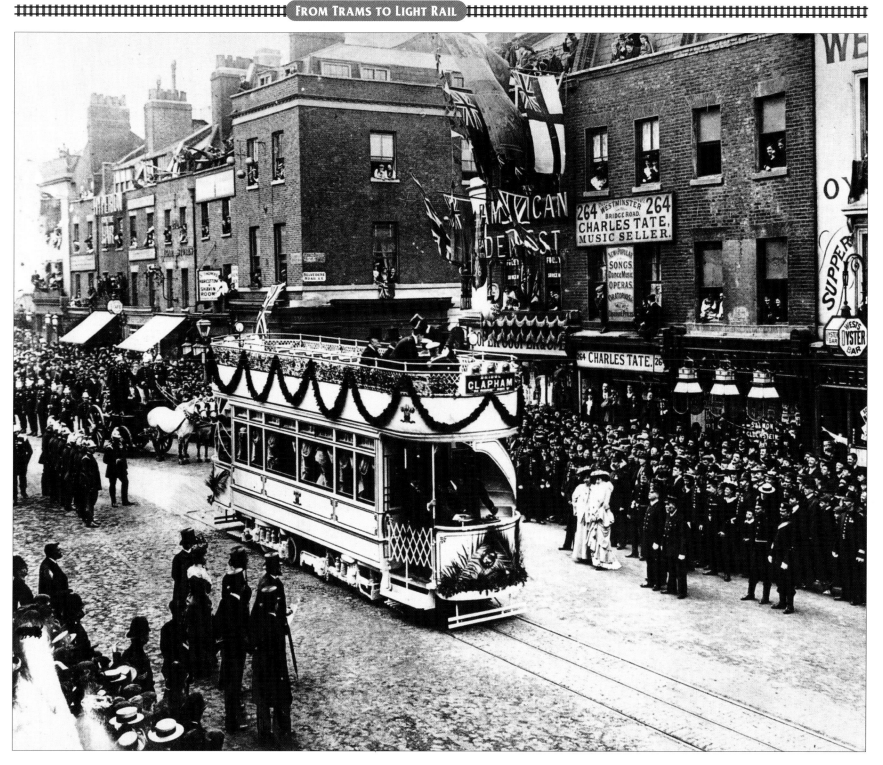

improved insulation and greater power – to 65bph in many cases – the motors became more compact, and the builders were able to use smaller wheels, which in turn lowered the platform and made it easier for passengers to board and dismount. Yet even for the most powerful trams, a low-tech 600-volt DC supply proved perfectly adequate for their relatively modest requirements.

Fares on the new electric trams were less than a half those charged on horse-drawn trams, and they proved an incomparable means of moving masses of people to work in the enormous factories of the era, or to those other destinations popular among working-class males in their leisure hours: football matches. They were used by both sexes, though still largely by the working classes, for shopping, often decked out at Christmas time with rows of electric lights. According to Winstan Bond, the electric tram 'represents for the average person the beginning of the mobility which we now take as a birthright with the motor car'.

Nowhere was this truer than in London, which was slow to introduce trams because the leases granted to the horse tramway companies didn't begin until the first years of the twentieth century. But then a complete tramway system was swiftly built, first by private companies, and then by the London County Council, which deliberately geared the routes to take people from newly built housing estates to their places of work (the first line terminated at an estate in Tooting). As a result, the number of workmen's tickets available at cut prices but generally valid only outside middle-class working hours soared from 582,000 in 1903, the last year of horse-drawn travel, to 3.34 million in 1906–1907. The result was a social transformation. One Edwardian records: 'We have fast lines of electric trams, brilliantly lighted, hurrying us down from over the bridges at half the time expended under the old conditions. Each workman today in the district has had an hour added to his life – half an hour actually saved from the transit and half an hour given back to him in the transit . . . family after family are evacuating the blocks of crowded tenements for little four-roomed cottages.'[3] Moreover, the competition forced the

By 1910 east London was being served by a bewildering variety of public transport, trams, horse buses, and the first 'General' motor buses.

LONDON'S TRAMWAYS

CHRISTMAS SHOPPING
TAKE AN ALL-DAY
1/- TICKET

railway companies south of the Thames to improve their own services and keep their fares down. However, there was a catch. The tramlines could not penetrate into the centre of London because the streets were simply too narrow and crooked, and the anti-tram forces, for whom the vehicles were a symbol of proletarian travel, too powerful. As a result, the centre of London was served exclusively by buses, and what Bond calls the 'blighted void' of the West End was a major tram-free zone. This left the trams very vulnerable to an assault by the motorbus in the 1920s.

The reminiscences of veterans reinforce the notion that working on the tramways, like virtually every other occupation open to the urban working classes between the wars, was a hard life.

> All the world knows what you are
> Conductor of a tramway car
> Alas poor wretch for little pay
> You work for fifteen hours a day
> I often wonder that a man
> Can spend his days upon a tram.

Youngsters would start work at the age of fourteen, drying the sand required to stop the trams slipping on gradients, or pouring water over the tracks in hot weather for twelve hours at a stretch to stop the tracks buckling. Discipline was strict: the straps of the uniforms had to be blackened; white collars had to be worn; boots had to be shiny. And you couldn't sign on if you weren't wearing a tie. If a man turned up a minute late he lost the job for the day. Yet unlike most workers of the time, the tram men benefited from a guaranteed eight-hour day, although they had to work right through without any meal breaks, 'brewing up' on the job.

One veteran conductor on the Isle of Man (where they were known as 'guards'), Arty Walmsley, remembers that he was not allowed to talk to the driver and wasn't even permitted time off to attend the christening of one of his children. 'There was no work around at the time. Work on the tramway wasn't glamorous – it was just work.' The trams were usually double-deckers carrying up to 100 passengers, and this meant carting around a lot of dirty, heavy old pennies, which soon blackened the guards' fingers.

Seventy-three-year-old former conductor Elsie Gallimore recalls problems with the inspectors, who would fine her if the tram was displaying the wrong destination at the front (on old trams the board would often slip). The conductor was in charge of the tram, and for a shy and frightened girl it was hard and tense work. Elsie suffered from terrible vertigo and would get into a panic about changing the trolley at the end of each journey.

The Second World War made life even harder, not least because of the blackout. As she remembers: 'In the dark people used to try to get away with giving you foreign coins or bits of metal. The inspectors were horrible, very strict.' Elsie had to pay any lost fares. In peacetime, the proliferation of special fares enabled both conductors and passengers to cheat, using cigarettes as bribes.

The tram had reached its peak just after the First World War, before the development of the modern motor bus. In 1920 there were 2,600 miles (4,184km) of tramway in Britain, carrying the amazing total of 48 billion passengers a year, and by 1927 there were nearly 15,000 tramcars. It was in the 1930s that the first symptoms of decline emerged. Towns and cities spread more widely, providing catchment areas better suited to the more flexible motor bus than to the tram, which came into its own in crowded city centres. Moreover, the popularity of what the commissioner of the Metropolitan Police had called an 'anachronism of the streets' was waning.

As a symbol of the urban past, the tram was naturally an early victim of the blitz conducted by the planners of Britain's town and city centres in the three decades after the war. The tramways were terribly vulnerable: their infrastructure had been battered by the war and neglected thereafter, and fares had been maintained at an increasingly uneconomic level.

Left: **A gleaming new tramway station at Douglas in the Isle of Man, the only part of the United Kingdom to have remained completely faithful to trams for more than a century.**

Opposite: **Despite attempts to persuade potential passengers that trams were an upmarket means of transport, they remained an essentially working-class phenomenon.**

Even before the war, new equipment was by no means advanced – in one euphemistic phrase, the trams used in Ilford were described as having been made 'with well-tried components'. 'Such modern-looking cars as were built,' notes Bond, 'were spread over a thirty-year period and clustered in tiny ghettos known only to the enthusiast.' The memory of one former passenger is typical: 'Travelling on the trams in Manchester was a very ramshackle experience . . . you sat there feeling very chilly, swaying with the movement of the tram. (Many of them were still being built with open tops.)

Worse was the backward-looking mentality of the managers. As P. J. Robinson, Liverpool's chief electrical engineer, stated in a controversial speech in 1936: 'The whole industry had to blame the 1910 mind of the average tramway manager for the fact that so many of the trams had fallen into disrepute, and they had to compare them with the 1935 minds of the bus people.' By contrast, in the United States, the standard PCC trams, designed under the auspices of the President's Conference Committee, were giving many tramway systems a new lease of life.

Nevertheless, some boroughs were still ordering trams after the war, and indeed, the final extension of the Leeds system was brought into operation as late as 1949. But the same year saw the last tram run in Manchester, and by 1962 there were only two surviving systems. Elsewhere, by and large, the tram was remembered not with nostalgia, but as a slow and noisy beast, trundling through the streets at an average speed of under 9mph (14.5kph). 'Noise was the chief grumble,' says one veteran of the trams. 'The crash when a tram hit the points of a loop, the clanging of the gongs, the rumbling and vibration.'

Over the next thirty years, trams survived in two locations, both, by no coincidence, places closely connected with the holiday habits of the northern working classes. The first, of course, was Blackpool, whose trademark trams still run along the promenade in a physical manifestation of the resort's special appeal. Yet this old-fashioned image is unfair and misleading, and not just because Blackpool has continued to thrive while many other British resorts have given up the ghost. The town has often been in the vanguard of change. In 1879, Blackpool had become the first town in Britain to employ the newly invented electric lights to power decorative illuminations. Indeed, the famous Blackpool Illuminations retain their appeal to this day. They provide a powerful attraction for hordes of visitors in months where they would otherwise be deterred by the advent of the dark, Lancastrian winter.

And in 1885, the electric lights were complemented by another innovation: construction of what was proudly described as the first tramway to be worked safely in the street by electricity (to be precise, a conduit groove between the rails). Despite early problems with high tides and sand in the conduit grooves, the system grew and flourished. In the 1930s, Walter Luff, the system's general manager, introduced 115 streamlined trams of a number of designs, including thirteen Luxury Dreadnoughts to run along the promenade. Luff's enthusiasm was an exception in a business which elsewhere was showing very few signs of life. As Winstan Bond puts it: 'Only Blackpool, by having a large proportion of good-looking trams and reserved tracks exposed to holidaymakers, achieved any mental impact,' or, in other words, were associated with a clean, modern form of transport.

The town continued to invest in the tram system after the war, but its fate was probably sealed, not only by the ever-increasing speed and comfort of the motor bus, but also by the new 'Coronation trams' introduced in the 1950s. These were a disaster: they were heavy, difficult to control and, worse, they were shoddily made, springing leaks from the start. By the end of the decade, the spirit seemed to have gone out of the council's defence of their trams. In 1960, it decided it could not afford to modernize the track (and it was in dire need of improvement – by then one section was known as the Wall of Death because of its circuitous route and the danger of the tram coming off the rails at any moment). By 1963 the system had completely run down. Yet not only was it the first system to be built and the last to go, but two routes survived: the one along the promenade and the more ambitious section along the coast to neighbouring Fleetwood. Their longevity is a tribute to Blackpool's unique capacity to retain and modernize attractions which date back to the late nineteenth century.

But even in Blackpool the tram survived only as a tourist attraction. The one remaining spot in Britain where it still fulfils its original role – that of a civic institution serving not just visitors but the whole community – is on the Isle of Man. Moreover, the island also boasts the only surviving – and prospering – horse-drawn tramway in the country. It's a 2-mile (3km) route along the promenade at Douglas, which opened in 1876 and has been in continuous use ever since (apart from a couple of years in the Second World War). It

has always been profitable, and by the 1920s it was carrying over 1.5 million passengers a year. The only visible change is that the tramway's forty-two horses, like the coachmen and conductors, work shorter hours than they once did. Today they are asked to do only four round trips daily, half their former mileage, and they know the form so well that they automatically stop at their stables after their fourth trip. And nowadays, when their careers are over, they are assured of being cared for in their retirement.

The Manx Electric Railway, which celebrated its centenary in 1993, is also extremely picturesque. It retains some of its

The famous horse-drawn trams running along the promenade at Douglas have not changed greatly since this photo was taken in 1926, except that the horses have to do a lot less mileage.

original cars and the majority of its track follows the coastline, providing passengers with some spectacular views. Two years after the electric railway was built, the enterprising Manxmen opened a branch from Laxey up to the 2,000ft (610m) peak of Snaefell. This route still uses five of its original cars, although in 1977 they were remotorized using units discarded by the city of Aachen.

The Manx trams have always been special, but there are those who remember the old days with something less than dewy-eyed nostalgia. Evelyn Frazer, who used to be a waitress at Snaefell, says the smell of disinfectant wafting through the newly washed trams used to make her feel sick. Even so, Evelyn, who has visited railways from Peru to South Africa, describes Laxey as 'the most beautiful station in the world'.

Blackpool's fabled illuminations usually feature its famous trams, duly lit up for the occasion.

Manchester's Metrolink, a triumphant, if long-delayed, example of municipal enterprise.

The Manx trams have always integrated the community, and they still offer a delivery service (for the record, it costs £1 ($1.50) to have an exhaust pipe delivered across the island). In its heyday the tramway also owned five pubs and the tramwaymen were noted for their enjoyment of life – Arty Walmsley recalls that they were supposed to be teetotal but most of them drank anyway and were often plied with drink by female holidaymakers.

When the tram was resurrected in the 1980s, it was as 'light rail' – a trendier, and in some ways more accurate term. The pioneering example of a modern railway system was built on Tyneside, although strictly speaking this was neither a tramway nor a light-rail network but a 'conurbational railway system' – a combination of the linking up and modernization of existing rail routes, with some new construction. It proved to be more expensive to create than had been originally envisaged, but it set an exciting precedent for maximizing the potential of existing rail systems by integrating them with each other and with a city's bus services.

So the honours for the first proper light-rail system went to Manchester, a modern justification of the old slogan 'What Manchester does today, the rest of the country does tomorrow.' Indeed, although lots of smaller towns had abandoned the tram in the 1930s, Manchester was the first major city to do so. The Manchester Corporation took this decision in 1946, by which time it owned three times as many buses as trams. So it was that on 10 January 1949, a convoy of five trams processed on their final journey to the depot amid, it has to be said, scant evidence of weeping, wailing, let alone gnashing of teeth, among the spectators.

It took forty-three years for railed transport to be restored to the streets of Manchester. The pro-rail battle began in the 1960s with plans, eventually aborted after ten years of effort on the grounds of cost, for the 'Pic-Vic' line. This was a proposed underground railway based, as its name implies, on the need to connect two of the city's three main railway stations, Piccadilly and Victoria.

The present Metrolink is the product of another ten-year battle. A joint railway study group was set up in 1982 in the wake of a spate of inner-city riots, notably those in the Toxteth district of nearby Liverpool in the summer of 1981. For there is an obvious connection between urban discontent and the availability of cheap and convenient mass transport to get people to work. The 1964 riots in the Watts district of Los Angeles can be traced back to the ripping up three years earlier of the tramways that had taken its inhabitants to work. The efforts of the 1980s were designed to restore to Manchester's reputation as 'capital of the north', and to a great extent this aim was achieved. The system that emerged linked some new lines and some stretches of roads through the city centre with a ramshackle collection of railway lines, mostly electrified.

The delays were seemingly endless, and after the long, drawn-out Pic–Vic fiasco the people of Manchester were decidedly sceptical. Even the Act of Parliament required took four years to get through because of a number of objections (including one from a supposedly pro-railway pressure group still yearning for the construction of Pic–Vic). Then another couple of years were spent navigating the bureaucratic obstacles placed in the path of any public-sector capital investment programme.

At last, in 1992, four years after the legislative go-ahead was given, the Metrolink was opened, running from Altrincham, south of the city, to Bury to the north. Inevitably, compromises had to be made. Low-level trams (which allow passengers to board without having to step up from the pavement) proved too expensive and had to be ruled out, and the cars themselves had to be made abroad, in Italy, because Britain had long ago lost the tram habit, and because no British manufacturer (especially Lord Weinstock, the ultra-cautious financier who ran the obvious candidate, GEC) wanted to take the risk.

In spite of the problems encountered at the planning stage, the new system soon became indispensable. In December 1994 the first derailment produced total chaos, as did an occasion when the wires froze. Passenger numbers doubled from a first-year total of 7 million, thanks to the Metrolink's 98 per cent reliability and its ability to reach 50mph (80kph) on the outer stretches and up to 30mph (48kph) in the centre of the city. Today the system has even been able to afford to restore one of the old trams, which was discovered being used as a home, complete with cooker and toilet, by a man in Huddersfield.

Like Manchester, Sheffield, the second city to install a new light-rail route, had a proud tram tradition – in the 1930s its trams ran on special tracks separated from the rest of the traffic, even in the city centre. Unfortunately, its modern-day equivalent, built soon after Manchester's, has not proved nearly as successful. Sheffield did not have Manchester's unique transport hollow in the city centre, and consequently lacked the same volume of potential passengers waiting for the service. The routes were awkward, with far less smooth, speedy and unimpeded travel on former rail lines than Manchester's system, and thus involved much more slow running through the streets. Moreover, the routes chosen were decided more by the heart than the head. In an effort to recreate the social benefits associated with the former LCC network, the burghers of Sheffield extended the lines to depressed parts of the city. It was a laudable intention, but unfortunately these areas have generated very little traffic since there was so little work available. Even so, within a decade Sheffield, like Manchester today, will be doubtless wondering how the city ever managed without its light-rail services.

An even more intriguing development in the renaissance of the tram is that the third new system under construction is to be based in Croydon, 10 miles (16km) south of central London, a prosperous borough which houses one of the biggest, and ugliest, collection of postwar offices anywhere in Britain. Since the town doesn't have the same tramway tradition as Manchester or Sheffield, Croydon Tramlink is a particularly imaginative scheme. As with the others, most of the tracks – 11 out of 17 miles (17 out of 28km), to be precise – will run either on or beside existing tracks, and there will be only a small on-street section in central Croydon itself, which will run either 'in protected public-transport lanes or in traffic-calmed streets'. The project will link central Croydon, which enjoys a superb rail service to central London, to its whole hinterland, from Wimbledon in the west to a major satellite housing estate at New Addington in the east.

Like its provincial brothers, the Croydon Tramlink, based on studies carried out in the 1980s, has taken a long time to come to fruition. The necessary legislation took four years to get through Parliament and it will not be opened until 2000, at a cost of £200 million ($300 million) for 17 miles (28km) of track. In the context of the rivalry between rail and road, it should be noted that this is lower than the cost of the Limehouse Link, a mere 1½ miles (2.5km) of road linking the City and Docklands. The tramlink will be operated by the consortium which won the tender to design, build and operate the scheme – a far cry from the municipal initiatives of the early years of the century. Despite the differences between the Croydon scheme and past systems, the fact that it is a major new initiative in an area without a tradition of tramway operation means that 'Today Croydon, tomorrow the world,' if not the world's most euphonious slogan, is nonetheless a justified one.

The Manx electric railway provides a service for most of the Isle of Man.

CHAPTER NINE

NOT JUST TOYS

TO THE BRITISH PUBLIC in general and train-lovers in particular, the words 'narrow gauge' summon up visions of holiday journeys on Welsh mountainsides or along southern beaches. But this is only a part of the story: outside the British Isles there are many narrow-gauge railways of 1m (3.3ft) or less which are the lifeblood of communities in mountains and forests. Such lines are not only able to tackle curves and gradients inaccessible to larger lines, they are also far cheaper to build.

Once there were dozens of them in Britain. They included a great many lines within gasworks and other 'industrial' lines, like the 2ft 6in- (770mm-) gauge line which served a paper mill at Kemsley in Kent until the 1960s. In the First World War, the Royal Engineers built literally hundreds of small lines to supply the trenches in France. Other examples of what might be described as 'miniature' railways, with gauges of little more than 1ft (305mm) were to be found in parks, or in the grounds of country estates. Indeed, the biggest mansions, like the Duke of Westminster's Eaton Hall in Cheshire, required what amounted to a small industrial railway.

Of the classic small lines, the narrowest is the Fairbourne Railway, set above the coast of north-west Wales. This was originally constructed in 1867 as a tramway to carry materials to build Barmouth Bridge and a row of terraced houses. It was then bought by Mr McDougall (of self-raising flour fame), who pressed it into service to transport materials from his own brickworks to build a resort in Barmouth. In 1916, the gauge was narrowed to 15ins (385mm). Appropriately enough, the trains used for passengers were supplied by Bassett–Lowke, best known for their miniature and toy trains. And in 1986 the gauge was narrowed even further, to a mere 12¼ins (314mm) and the railway became purely a tourist line.

The Fairbourne was unusual in terms of its cargo, for most of the other serious (that is, industrial) lines in the area were built to carry slate for roofing from the Welsh hills to the sea and thence the length and breadth of Britain, a demand which exploded during the building boom of the mid-nineteenth century. The history of many of these railways follows a certain pattern. Often they were founded before the arrival of steam power and converted to steam during the mid-nineteenth century, abandoned in the twenty-five years after the Second World War and rescued by heroic bands of enthusiasts thereafter.

One of the west Wales railways, the 2ft 6in- (770mm-) gauge Welshpool and Llanfair Light Railway, was a more or less ordinary line. Its nickname, the Farmers' Line, sums up its original role. It carried heavy goods of every description – livestock, timber, coal and fertilizer – as well as passengers. As it ran through the streets it could drop travellers right outside their homes – indeed, it was said that hanging washing often had to be taken down to allow the train through. Like many of its contemporaries, it was closed for passengers in 1931, taken over by BR in 1948, closed for goods eight years later and revived in 1960, albeit to operate only weekend trains.

A classic 0–6–0 goods engine beside Lake Padarn in north Wales. This veteran, built by Hunslet in 1882, is carrying a load of slate on the 4-foot (1,231mm) gauge Padarn Railway from Llanberis to Port Dinorwic.

In the early days of railways, designers were looking for the broadest possible gauge to accommodate the largest boilers they could, and it was generally assumed that genuinely narrow-gauge railways, of below 1m (3.3ft) in width, were impracticable. This belief was triumphantly disproved by the Festiniog Railway, which had opened in north Wales in 1836 as a horseway to the same gauge – 23½ins (597mm) – as that used in the quarries. This was wide enough to allow the horses to pull wagons efficiently but sufficiently narrow to cope with the sharp mountain curves. The Festiniog runs on the same gauge to this day. In the early 1860s proper railway tracks were built by Charles Spooner, the son of James Spooner, an engineer who had settled in the area after holidaying there. In 1863, the first steam trains started to haul slate from the mountains round Blaenau Festiniog to Port

No, this is not the author at home. It is the retired manager of the Festiniog Railway posing by the side of an abandoned coach from his beloved line.

Madoc, and the next year the Board of Trade gave the Festiniog Railway permission to run a passenger service. It was the first such licence ever granted to a narrow-gauge railway.

Spooner's next innovation was a more powerful engine, the famous 'double bogie' devised by Robert Fairlie. This locomotive, aptly named *Little Wonder*, looked like two back to back, but in fact it was a single engine with a long boiler resting on two separate bogies. The fire boxes and driver's platform (in those days there was no nonsense about a cab) were centrally mounted. This idea, used in most of today's diesel and electric locomotives, provided enough power to prevent the line having to be doubled to carry the traffic. In 1873 the same bogie principle was applied to passenger coaches and goods wagons on the line, and these were among the first iron-framed bogie coaches in the world.

When Spooner died in 1889, he left the rights to his innovations to the railway itself. The revenue was certainly needed, because by then mainline railways had reached Blaenau Festiniog, and the narrow-gauge railway therefore became the first of its type to have to rely solely on passenger traffic. It did well enough to be able to take over and complete work on the ill-fated Welsh Highland Railway between Caernarfon and Port Madoc in 1923. Construction had been started in 1875 but had never been finished. During the war the rails were therefore taken away for scrap and only now is the Festiniog – which itself went out of business in 1946 and was restarted nine years later – putting the Highland line back together again.

Spooner was not the first person to convert a horseway in north Wales. For centuries slate had been mined in the hills above the Irish Sea, and the first 'railroad' to replace the previous cumbersome and uneconomic combination of carts and narrowboats had been built by Lord Penrhyn in 1801 as a tramway from his quarries at Bethesda to Port Penrhyn. By the 1820s this had been laid with conventional rails. At one time the Penrhyn quarry was the largest in the world. At its peak it had 600 wagons on the outside line and a further 2,000 in the quarry itself.

The first stretch of the 2' 7½" (808mm) Snowdon Mountain Railway after it leaves Llanberis is relatively flat, but nonetheless picturesque for all that.

At around the same time an English immigrant, Sir Thomas Assheton-Smith, followed suit with a 9-mile (14.5-km) line from the quarries over 2,500ft (762m) up on Elidir Mountain to Port Dinorwic on the Menai Strait. In the early 1840s this was replaced after a 4ft- (1,230mm-) gauge railway, its points supported by huge slate slabs, had been laid on a route alongside Lake Padarn, by which time over 60 tons of slate were being carried daily in trains worked by a combination of gravity and animal power.

Smith's son Tom was fascinated by steam power. Like most of the other railway-builders, he was inspired by the pioneers. Indeed, the early tracks were often brought from Newcastle, and known as 'Newcastle roads'. Tom Smith already owned a number of steam yachts when he ordered two steam locomotives in 1848. In due course, Tom's second son and successor ordered locomotives with vertical boilers named after his racehorses (*King of the Scarlets* and *Lady Madcap* were two) for use in the family's mine. This was enormous, covering 700 acres (283 hectares), and boasted over twenty galleries – the faces where the slate was mined – each with its own locomotive. Life for the 3,000 workers was by no means easy, especially since many of them suffered from silicosis, as veterans of the last days of the quarry in the 1960s still do. Although the official language in the mine was English, in typical Welsh fashion they formed their own community, their own civilization. The miners were copious readers, to such an extent that the quarry was almost a working man's university.

The Smiths' Padarn Railway was closed in October 1961. The rails were scrapped, the fittings preserved and, eight years later, the quarry and its railway were abandoned altogether. The line was reopened in 1972 as an adjunct to Padarn, a country park which houses the National Slate Museum of Wales.

Above: **The Isle of Man can be bleak and beautiful – the 1.45pm service from Ramsey crossing Glen Mooar Viaduct.**

Opposite: *Michael* **coming to help** *King of the Scarlets* **– two of the engines on the extremely narrow (1' 10¾"/ 583mm)-gauge Dinorwic Quarry Railway.**

The first of the many such slate railways to be saved for posterity was the Talyllyn, a typical line built in the 1860s to a 2ft 6in- (770m-) gauge and used to move slate from quarries at Bryn Eglws to the coast at Tywyn. The quarry closed in 1946 and the line four years later, but it was only a year before it was reopened as the first preserved railway in the world, thanks to the enthusiasm – and the cash – of Tom Rolt. Understandably, the Talyllynites like to think of their line not as a museum piece but as a direct continuation of the original one.

In some places, by contrast, there are still native quarries, and there internal railways still at work even though the external line has been abandoned. The classic case is the Aberllefeni quarry, which formerly depended on the 2ft 3in- (692mm-) gauge Corris Railway to Machynlleth. This was closed in 1948 and is only now being resurrected by the owners of the Talyllyn Railway.

Most of these reopened lines are manned largely, or completely, by volunteers. Not so the 12-mile-long (19km) Vale of Rheidol Railway, built in the early years of the century to a tiny 1ft 11in- (590mm-) gauge. This has a permanent paid staff, though in other respects its history is typical enough. In 1930 the line stopped carrying freight and relied only on summertime passenger services. And in 1988, this last outpost of steam on BR's network was sold to a private company.

North Wales is also the site of one of the first narrow-gauge railways to be used purely to transport tourists. This climbs to within 100ft (30m) of the summit of Snowdon, taking an hour to carry fifty-nine passengers the 4 miles (6km) to this point. The rack-and-pinion line, with a gauge of 2ft 7¼ins (800mm), which was opened in 1896, was based on the technology developed by the Swiss for more ambitious lines in the Alps. It reflected the belief that persists in many places to this day that no holiday was complete without a ride on a miniature train. A decade earlier Magnus Volk had opened the first electric railway in Britain – along the Brighton seafront. This remains the most interesting and original of the many such lines designed to carry holidaymakers along promenades or seemingly endless piers.

On Snowdon even the smallest accident can look dramatic in the mountain's habitual mist. This engine had run into the empty carriages of an earlier train in 1896.

The most publicized, the busiest, the most delightful of all Britain's narrow-gauge railways: the Romney Hythe and Dymchurch on the Kent Coast with its Pacific locomotives one third the size of the real-life, grown-up original.

A symbol of defiance, a miniature armoured train on the Romney Hythe and Dymchurch Railway defying German aircraft during the Second World War.

Of all these lines, the Romney Hythe and Dymchurch, along the coast of southern Kent, is the best known, the most useful and the least typical – as well as being one of the narrowest, with a gauge of a mere 15ins (385mm). It is the best known because it is the longest, at 13½ miles (21.7km) and the closest to London; the most useful because its trains carry not only 150,000 tourists a year but also the local inhabitants, and it is the least typical because its origins lie, not in unglamorous industrial logic, but in the grandest of gestures.

Its founder was one Captain J. E. P. Howey, a millionaire who had inherited a great deal of property in Melbourne, Australia. In the early 1920s, following the death of his great friend Count Louis Zborowski in a motor race, Howey took over the responsibility for two Pacific-type locomotives built by Davey Paxman to a scale of about a third of the original.

He instructed the locomotives' designer, Henry Greenly, to find a site for a track on which to run them, and Greenly came up with the Kent coast. Howey, not one for bureaucracy, had already started to build the line six months before he got the official go-ahead. Before Greenly left in 1928 after a row with Howey, he had supervised the construction of proper bogie coaches, generally reckoned to be the best ever made for a small-scale line. Two later locomotives were judged to be more North American in design and appearance than the original Pacific.

The line was an immediate success, helped by Howey's insouciance and his fondness for driving one of the locomotives himself, his trousers held up by Old Etonian braces. On the outbreak of war in 1939 the line was requisitioned as it was the only means of transport along a stretch of coast particularly exposed to German bombs – and to a German invasion. The most famous image of its role in the war was as the world's only miniature armoured train, formed of two hopper wagons modified to carry Lewis guns and an antitank rifle. It became a symbol of Britain's David-like defiance of the German Goliath; indeed, stories abounded of how the railway's tiny size was in fact its best defence. German bombers would fly overhead, and, so the legend goes, seeing the tiny tracks, the pilots would think they were further from the ground than they actually were, fly even lower and crash into the ground. Equally symbolic was the reopening of the line in 1946 by Stan Laurel and Oliver Hardy, no less. It was a sign that Britain was back to normal.

Unfortunately, when Howey died in 1963, his widow was unenthusiastic about financing the considerable refurbishments required to the track, the trains and the stations, especially as the growth of foreign holidays had rather reduced its appeal. After a couple of subsequent owners had found the burden too much, it was rescued in 1971 by a consortium headed by a worthy successor to Howey: 'Bill' McAlpine, a well-known train-lover, and one wealthy enough to be able to restore the line to its original glory.

SOURCES

2 WHY RAILWAYS?

1. Gourvish, T.R.: *British Railways 1948-73, A Business History* (Cambridge University Press, 1986).

3 THE PIONEERS

1. Faith, Nicholas: *The World the Railways Made* (The Bodley Head, London, 1990). The source of all unattributed quotations in Chapters 3 and 4.
2. Ransom, John: *The Victorian Railway and How it Evolved* (Heinemann, London, 1990).
3. Rolt, L.T.C.: *George and Robert Stephenson* (Longman, London, 1960).
4. Rowland, John: *George Stephenson, Railway Pioneer* (Lutterworth Press, Cambridge, 1971).
5. John Ransom, op. cit.
6. L.T.C. Rolt, op. cit.

4 THE MIRACULOUS DECADES

1. Francis, John: History of the English Railway (Dragonwheel Books, Pulborough, 1996).
2. Biddle, Gordon: *Great Railway Stations of Britain* (David & Charles, Newton Abbott, 1986).
3. Reed, M.C.: *Investment in Railways in Britain* (Oxford University Press, Oxford, 1975).
4. Lewin, Henry Grote: *The Railway Mania and its Aftermath* (David & Charles, Newton Abbott, 1968).
5. John Francis, op. cit.
6. John Francis, op. cit.
7. Lambert, R.S.: *The Railway King* (Allen & Unwin, London, 1934).

5 SPEED IS THE ESSENCE

1. Wilson, C. David: *Racing Trains: The 1895 Railway Races to the North* (Alan Sutton, Stroud, 1995).

2. Nock, O.S.: *Speed Records on Britain's Railways* (David & Charles, Newton Abbott, 1971).
3. Quoted in O.S. Nock, op. cit.
4. Fiennes, Gerald: *I Tried to Run a Railway* (Ian Allan, Shepperton, 1967).

6 FROM COAL TO CONTAINERS

1. Robbins, Michael: *The Railway Age* (Routledge & Keegan Paul, London, 1962).
2. Quoted by G.R. Hawke in *Railways and Economic Growth in England and Wales* (Oxford University Press, 1970).
3. Morgan, Bryan: *Express Journey 1864-1964, A Centenary of the Express Dairy Company Ltd* (Published for the EDCL by Neame, 1964).
4. Bonavia, Michael: *History of the Southern Railway* (Unwin Hyman, London, 1987).
5. Rhodes, Michael: *The Illustrated History of British Marshalling Yards* (Haynes Publishing, Yeovil, 1989).

7 MOVING THE MASSES

1. Quoted in *Labyrinths of Iron* by Benson Bobrick (Newsweek Books, New York, 1981).
2. Michael Bonavia, op. cit.
3. Baker, Michael: *The Southern Electric Story* (Silver Link Publishing, Peterborough, 1993).

8 FROM TRAMS TO LIGHT RAIL

1. Holt, David: *Manchester Metrolink* (Platform 5 Publishing, Sheffield, 1992).
2. Winstan Bond, A.: *The British Tram: History's Orphan* (The Tramway Museum Society, Crich, 1980).
3. Quoted in *Moving Millions* by Theo Barker (London Transport Museum, 1990).

INDEX

Picture Acknowledgements

Alison Hargreaves Associates: 118; Barry Flaxman: 104; The Bass Museum: 80 (left); The Bridgeman Art Library: 18, 20, 21, 22, 26, 33, 35, 37, 38, 39, 40-41, 42, 47, 50-51, 78-79, 90, 99, 102, 114; English, Welsh and Scottish Railway Limited: 87; E.T. Archive: 29, 52; Eurostar (U.K.) Ltd: 14, 72; Hulton Getty Picture Collection: 16, 24, 28, 32, 36, 44, 48, 49, 56, 60-61, 64, 65, 68, 74, 82, 84-85, 92, 93, 96, 97, 100-101, 103, 110, 113, 116-117, 119, 121, 125; The Image Bank: 123; Images Colour Library: 58, 70 (left), 122; Imperial War Museum: 136; The Ivo Peters Collection: 8-9, 62, 76, 77, 126, 129, 130, 131; Life File: 23; Mary Evans Picture Library: 1, 10, 31, 45, 46, 95, 98, 105, 112, 115; National Railway Museum/Science & Society Picture Library: 2-3, 54, 55, 66, 67, 69, 71, 80 (right), 81, 83; Topham Picture Library: 12-13, 70 (right), 86, 88-89, 94, 106-107, 134-135; National Library of Wales: 128, 132-133.